TO GUARD MY *Every* NEIGHBOR

Copyright © 2016 by Keith Schneider

All rights reserved. No part of this book may be reproduced in any form by any electronic or mechanical means including photocopying, recording, or information storage and retrieval without permission in writing from the author.

ISBN: 978-0-996653152
LCCN: 2016936614

Cover Photography by Lea Taubinger
Book Design by Logotecture

First Edition

Printed in the U.S.A.

Writestream Publishing, LLC
Parker Ford, PA
writestreampublishing.com

DEDICATION

First of all, thank you, God, for making it possible for me to do what I love to do.

    Thank you to my parents, John and Grace Schneider, for believing in me. To my little brother Peter, and older brother John, thank you for being there. Special thanks to my daughter Kierston (a.k.a. "Shitbag"). To my boys Arturo Rodriguez, Steve Spinizola, Jose Castro, Polo, Station 47 B, and all of my brothers and sisters working in the field, thanks for all you do. To Doc Arnold and Rob Logan, thank you for your friendship. Thank you, Michelle, for being there. To Omar and Damalis, thank you for connecting me with the right ghostwriter. Finally, to Daria Anne and Writestream Publishing, many thanks for bringing my story to life.

TO GUARD MY *Every* NEIGHBOR

Inside the Fire

Lt. Keith Schneider
with Daria Anne DiGiovanni

FOREWARD

I met Lieutenant Keith Schneider one autumn day last year when he knocked on my door to inquire about ghostwriting services. A mutual friend who was familiar with Writestream Publishing suggested he talk to me about his book for the purpose of bringing his incredible story to life. From that first interaction, I recognized the depth of his character and his desire to educate the public about the role of a fireman and what it truly entails.

When I read the old manuscript he'd entrusted me with, the one he'd written several years prior to our meeting, the calls he described were sobering. I am ashamed to say, I truly had no idea what first responders deal with on a daily basis, both on the street doing their jobs and inside the station, in terms of bureaucracy and politics.

Yes, I was raised to respect and appreciate the service of firemen, police, and paramedics, but until I worked on Keith's book, I did not have a genuine understanding of the toll it takes on a human being to effectively confront and manage the worst of human behavior and the most horrific of tragedies on a daily basis. For someone like him to have remained in this honorable line of work for 30 years – often at great sacrifice to his personal wellbeing and relationships – speaks volumes about the kind of man he is.

Learning about the long-lasting effects of PTSD and the inability to escape the "warzone" was also a wake-up call. I hope that after reading *To Guard My Every Neighbor: Inside the Fire*, private citizens will not only gain a deeper knowledge about first responders (and hopefully never again chide a fireman, cop, or paramedic with the words, "I pay your salary"), but also be inspired to offer meaningful assistance to those who have faithfully answered the call of duty in their communities.

Thank you, Keith, for your service and your willingness to share your experiences for the benefit of others.

Daria Anne DiGiovanni

Writestream Publishing, LLC

Writestream Radio Network

INTRODUCTION

I consider myself a New Yorker. And sometimes I consider myself a Floridian.

The middle child of three boys, I was born at Long Island Jamaican Hospital to John and Grace Schneider. I spent my first four years of life on Magnolia Avenue in Seldon on Long Island, until my dad's job transfer to Stuart operations for Gruman Aerospace, where he worked as an electrical engineer. I've lived in Florida ever since.

But I do love New York.

I had the best parents in the world. When we were growing up, we weren't rich, but they took good care of us and made sure we were involved in sports and everything else that makes for a great childhood. As I grew, my interests were raising hell with my brothers and going to school.

During my teenage years, I attended Fort Pierce Central High School, where I had a good time and participated on the swim team. Other than that, I didn't play too many sports, although I used to cut class all the time to surf. Some days, I'd get up at 4 a.m. for morning sessions before school. My father has since passed away, and my mom is now in a nursing home; I knew that was coming because I used to see it all the time when I worked as a fireman in Brevard County.

Out of high school, I probably had more jobs than the average person does in a lifetime. I worked for Luria's, a Miami-based retailer, building catalogue showrooms, along with another guy. I dug ditches for Roto-Rooter, a septic and sewer company. I worked for a landscape company, my last employer before I got the job as a fireman. Even while employed as a fireman, I worked for a stable company, digging out piss holes for horses. Talk about your *Dirty Jobs* – that one definitely could have been featured on Mike Rowe's show. Do you have any idea how much horse urine stinks? It was terrible.

So what made me decide to become a fireman?

I'd like to say I did it for heroic reasons, but the truth is, it's kind of a funny story. One night my buddy Donny Snyder and I were standing outside of my girlfriend's house talking about what we wanted to do. We were both tired of our jobs; I was working at Luria's, and he was a mechanic with Toyota. Then we heard sirens, and he turned to me and said, "Why don't we go do that?"

"Do what?" I asked.

"Why don't we go be firemen? They only work ten days a month. They work one day, and they're off two."

And I was like, "OK."

That evening, we drove to the college and signed up for the class. Once they accepted us, I had no idea what I'd just gotten into. I was completely blind to it. I didn't know a thing about being a fireman. I'd seen plenty of brush fires because we had them behind our house but other than that, I was clueless.

Once we got the books and started thumbing through them, we thought, "Wow, we never knew all this!"

Then school started and provided us with an eye-opening experience, which ultimately led me to a 30-year career. I started out as a volunteer fireman for the city of Stuart in Martin County until I was hired by Brevard County, otherwise known as the Space Coast and the home of the Kennedy Space Center. My first official day on the job was October 6, 1986. I was stationed on Merritt Island at the busiest house in the county, Station 23 (now 41). After working for 15 years in various stations around Brevard, I earned a promotion to lieutenant, something I'll discuss in greater detail later on.

Compared to a firefighter in a major metropolitan area like New York or Chicago, my experience is somewhat limited. However, with the same task at hand, every firefighter in the world has a singular purpose: to prevent the tragic loss of life.

In spite of our very best efforts, we cannot succeed one-hundred percent of the time. When the public calls out to the Fire Rescue Department, we as firefighters, emergency medical technicians, and paramedics must do more than what we've been trained for, and at times, go far beyond what can reasonably be expected of a normal person.

Yet in all respects, we are normal. Emergency personnel wear many other hats: a number of us are also electricians, carpenters, police officers, and plumbers. But most importantly, we are your comfort in your time of need, your friend when things go bad, and your shoulder to cry on when a loved one passes away.

When we begin our career in the Fire Department, they give us special gear designed to protect us from the extreme heat we must encounter in order to do our job. Made of Nomex and many other fine materials, it comes in an array of colors. I call it my suit of armor, my bunker gear. They even show us how to put it on properly.

The problem is, they never really show us how to take it off.

I'm writing this book for the purpose of giving taxpayers,

would-be firemen, and anyone who is simply curious about what we do an insider's perspective. I'll take you on some of the most horrific calls I've been on, from start to finish. You'll feel what I'm feeling and develop an understanding of how every call affects my daily life, from the moment I first arrive.

Although retired, I am a fireman forever, until I draw my last breath. I'm on 24 hours a day, seven days a week. Yes, we do bring our work home. We have no choice about what we see, smell, hear, or experience on any given call, and those impressions stay with us permanently. They embed themselves in our memory banks, never to be forgotten.

On the positive side, my life as a fireman has taught me to appreciate the blessings I've been given and the people I love, including a beautiful daughter who is now 29.

These days I like to play hockey because it helps me get some of the aggression out…at least when I get to fight, anyway. I founded the Wounded Warriors Hockey Club in 2014 to raise money for numerous veterans' charities.

I'm easygoing. I've learned that what you have today may be gone tomorrow so I'm thankful for everything that comes to me. I hope that after reading my story, the next time you see a fireman, you'll see what he sees, hear what he hears, and lives what he lives.

Lieutenant Keith Schneider

Indialantic Beach, Florida

PROLOGUE

If I Could
Merritt Island, Florida
January 18, 1992

I dream about the jet-ski. That's the one that gets to me.

I was on overtime at Station 41 on Merritt Island. On this sunny, cool day all of the other trucks were down at 43 for training, which meant we at 41 were covering the island. It had been fairly busy, with most calls ending with minor transports to the hospital. I was on duty with fire medic Charlie and volunteer Greg.

As Rescue 41 approached the station, the radio crackled, "Rescue 41 Control."

Charlie answered, "Rescue 41 Alma Boulevard. Go ahead."

"Rescue 41, respond in Engine 42's area, at the end of South Newfound Harbor Drive. Reference a jet-ski accident with injuries."

"Alright, let's go," I said as I turned the rig around to head in that direction. I was behind the wheel, with Charlie sitting next to me. Greg was in the back of the rig, looking at us through the pass way.

And I flew.

But my thoughts reverberated through my mind just as quickly: *Will I have to swim out to get them? How badly are they hurt?*

My heart began to pound in my chest. I could hear the siren winding; my foot felt heavy.

Charlie turned to Greg and ordered him to grab the C-spine equipment when we got there. Turning onto State Road 520, we encountered traffic congestion, forcing me to swerve in and out while cursing all of the bone-headed drivers who didn't know their right from their left. Finally, we weaved our way through and arrived at the scene – a house situated on the river in a well-to-do suburb.

As we approached the home, an adult out front informed us, "There's one in the bathtub; the other one's sitting out on the dock. We put a towel around her."

"OK," I acknowledged.

I grabbed some medical equipment and threw it on the stretcher. As I went through the backyard, I saw her sitting upright on the dock with her legs crossed; an older gentleman was holding her up. Charlie stopped to grab supplies while I walked out to her. I put one hand on her back and another in front of her as I got down on one knee and looked up at her face. When my eyes met hers, my heart sank. I noticed how young she was, with pale, white skin that was cool to the touch.

And her eyes. Her haunting eyes. How I will never forget them.

They were wide open, with huge pupils. I asked her a question, but there was no response. Nothing but a blank stare. Death had arrived, and he was here to take someone – someone whose life had not yet even begun.

"Charlie, it's not good," I announced. "We have a trauma code." By now, he was already setting up drugs and preparing her for CPR. Together, we laid her down on her back and moved her a bit for better access. I started to ventilate while Charlie stood by ready to intubate. At this point, I was standing in the shallow water. We immediately attempted CPR. There was no pulse; she wasn't breathing.

Charlie then informed me, "Hey, I'm gonna try and get the tube."

"OK."

But he couldn't get the tube in because the accident had forced her to clench her teeth. While he worked on her, he yelled at Greg to see how his patient was doing. She was fine. It was like a nightmare as I looked up and saw all of her friends standing around a house away, yelling for her to hold on. I grabbed the radio to advise Control we had a trauma code and to send us District Engine 43 and Rescue 43.

I got denied because they were all in training.

Again I repeated, "We need help."

Finally, after I called two or three more times, the Battalion Chief got on and asked, "What do you have?"

"We have a 14- year-old Class 1 and a 13-year-old Class 3. We need air care and with three people on the scene, we can't handle it ourselves."

The Battalion replied that all units would be responding just as Greg came back out to check with us since his patient was stable. When I began to ventilate again, the young girl started to vomit. We ignored the stench, suctioned, and continued our efforts. The smell was enough to gag, but we had work to do.

Death wasn't going to win this one, I swore to myself.

Charlie established two IV lines and began to push drugs, per our protocol. The AMBU bag became slippery due to the vomit on my hands, but I just kept wiping them on my pants as I focused on my task. We continued CPR. Then Charlie started the first (I.V.) line of saline. After five minutes, help began to arrive. When the Battalion Chief came on-scene, he saw exactly what was going on. In the meantime, Charlie kept trying to get the tube in, with no success, and the other Lieutenant set up command and the landing zone (L.Z.) for the forthcoming chopper.

Firefighter J.P. took my place with the ventilation so I could go inside and check on the other patient. As I entered the house, I was greeted by a group of young girls, friends of the victim, who peppered me with questions: *How is she? Is she going to be alright? Will she make it?*

Here I was, faced with ten teenagers. *Do I tell them?* I tried to speak, but no words would come out. Instead, I looked aside and brushed away the tears that had formed in my eyes. Although I said nothing, the look on my face provided their answer. My heart ached as I heard their gut-wrenching sobs, an acknowledgment that they understood the seriousness of their friend's condition.

I then helped Greg C-spine the other patient, who couldn't remember anything about the accident. When she and Greg inquired about the girl on the dock, I ignored the question and finished my work. When Rescue 241 arrived on the scene and took over, I headed back out to relieve J.P. on ventilation.

"Well I'll have to do a crike$_1$," the Chief announced, before ordering me to hyperventilate her. I did as I was told. The moment he made his first cut, her blood gushed out like a raging river, flowing through the cracks in the dock and hitting the water. I was covered in fluid as I struggled to hold the bag and wiped my hands on my pants.

I felt like I was in a time warp. Everything going on around me seemed to play out in slow motion; the voices I heard sounded as if I was listening to a tape on warped speed. When I stepped back to take a breath, I looked up and saw two adults running through the yard.

The first one I spotted through the fence was a lady who slid to her knees. I could hear her screaming at the top of her lungs, "No!"

Next, a man come through, wearing a blue satin jacket with a Fire Department emblem on it. And in that moment, I knew that he knew what we were doing was not good. He kept trying to approach, but I just continued to point at him with my bloody glove and tell him, "No."

"It's my daughter!" he yelled. He stopped next to his wife and fell to his knees.

In that moment, I knew that this is what he did for a living; that he fully understood what was going on; and that he was all too aware of what the end results usually are in many of these cases.

I gazed up at the heavens and asked, "God, why me? Why such a young girl? Why does it have to be a fellow firefighter's daughter?"

My pleas were interrupted by the sounds of a helicopter landing. I don't know how that pilot got it in there, but somehow he managed to land right in a little circular-shaped clearing, surrounded by palm trees.

Once we stabilized her enough, we loaded her onto the backboard and placed her on the stretcher for transport to the chopper. As we did, I whispered, "Please fight. Don't leave us." When we got her to the rig and loaded her up, I desperately wanted to accompany her. I didn't want to let her go. For some reason, I felt that if I could stay with her, she would live.

As the helicopter lifted off, so did a piece of me, never to return again.

Charlie and I returned to the dock to pick up the equipment. Anger erupted within me while I started throwing tubes into the bag. Then I looked at him and noticed the tears in his eyes. As we both began to cry, I stepped away and headed to the end of the dock where no one could see me.

I thought, *There's a hole in my armor. Firemen do not cry.*

Once I composed myself, I walked back to the equipment and carried it to the rescue units. Passing through the fence, I heard more crying, which caused my eyes to well up with tears again. I barely made it back to the rig before I broke down into uncontrollable sobbing. I just couldn't stop.

The next thing I knew, the Chief approached me and told me to report to the District's car: Charlie and I were relieved from duty for the rest of the shift. We had an impromptu briefing, but there was nothing much we could say. We got sent home. I slept in the vomit and blood-stained clothes on the floor, curled up in a fetal position.

Later, we got permission to go to the funeral, something first responders don't normally do. However, since this was a fellow firefighter's daughter and a young victim, they allowed us to attend for closure. Being there was just as emotionally charged as the call: we were surrounded by tons of her friends, all sobbing. When we saw her mother and father, they thanked us and said, "There was nothing more you could have done." Eventually, we learned that she died from a complete separation of the aorta from the heart, resulting in rapid and complete fluid loss.

The funny thing about running traumatic calls where there's a death is that you don't forget a face. You don't forget a sound. You don't forget the smell (the most dominant sense) of vomit, blood, radiator fluid, feces, and burning flesh and foliage. You don't forget the cries and screams you hear. You don't forget the feeling of holding a body that is so broken up, you can't really grab it because it's poured into your hands.

All these years later, I still see her face, hear the cries of her friends and relive those awful, helpless feelings. Some days, I don't think about it at all; other times, all I *can* do is think about it. When that happens, I constantly replay the events in my mind and wonder if we could have done anything differently. Every time, the answer is, "No."

That leads to another question, "Why am I still here?"

There is no answer to that one.

THE EARLY YEARS

"When everything goes to hell, the people who stand by you without flinching – they are your family."
– Jim Butcher

My dad's side is German; my mom's side is Italian. Our family was close with my maternal uncle's family, which included seven kids. They moved down to Florida and stayed with us for a short time until they bought their own house. We got together for special occasions and milestones like holidays, birthdays, and graduations. I loved being a part of it all. As time went on, that tradition and the closeness we shared just sort of floundered and disappeared. Although I didn't know it then, my family would eventually become the fire department.

As you might expect, my brothers and I were rambunctious boys. Whenever my mom was driving us around in the car, and someone was acting up, she'd look in the rearview mirror to determine who it was. Then she'd reach down, take off her shoe, and toss it backwards to hit the guilty party. Afterward, she'd ask for it back, and you had to give it to her. My mom was awesome.

Although I only attended Catholic school for a year, my brother and I were altar boys for a long time. Yes, I drank the altar wine. And I ate the hosts. We used to play tackle football with Father Culligan, who was a great guy, on the church grounds. But when we were doing the service, he was the one who poured the most wine into the cup. Then when it was time to add the water, he'd always put his finger over it to prevent it from diluting the wine.

Because Peter, John, and I loved to play football, inevitably, someone was always getting hurt. I broke my arm once and another time, my brother broke his arm *and* his leg. In the wake of each incident, my dad drove us to the hospital. While it may seem trivial to mention, I'll explain its relevance a little later in the story.

There were three boys who lived around the corner, Matt, Mark, and Mike Schneider (no relation to us). They lived on Wyoming; we lived on Newport Drive. They were the heavier-set, shorter guys and we were the skinny, tall guys. We'd go to the churchyard often to play football.

One day, somebody threw the ball at Peter and it broke his middle finger. Well, we had to do 11:30 a.m. mass the next day. If you've been raised Catholic, you know that when you do stuff as an altar boy, one guy has this job, the other has that job. Peter was the one who would get the Bible and hold it up as the priest read it. I didn't think about it during the service, but my mom told me that while Peter was holding the Bible, his middle finger was sticking straight up, so it looked like he was flicking everybody off in the church. I remember hearing her laughing in the back and not understanding why until she told me later.

HELL-RAISING AND HIGH SCHOOL

My first year of high school, in the ninth grade, I got all A's; I was doing *great*. Then, my brother John enticed me to do something in my sophomore year that became a habit. One morning he informed me, "Hey man, we're gonna skip school today."

And I was like, "OK."

"We're gonna show you how to do it," he added.

"OK," I agreed.

We caught the bus to school and got off in the bus zone. As soon as we hit the pavement, we turned and started walking to the railroad tracks out back behind school. Now, they were a good, long walk. You had to walk through PE (Physical Education) and the PE field was wide open; you had to make it all the way across. It felt like a desert. If it had been a concentration or prison camp, you'd be waiting to get shot in the back of the head. We walked and walked until we got on the other side of the tracks.

By now, I was like, "Man, we're not really going to school, are we?"

He answered, "No."

And I was like, "Alright."

As we approached the railroad tracks, we turned left to make it out to Oleander Ave., where there was, a car waiting. It had a bunch of chicks in it and another dude. My brother John and I climbed in. I was in the back.

Now, I wasn't the *ladies' man* in high school, so I didn't know what goes where and why and all that. Immediately, John started making out with one of the chicks, while the other chick was up front messing around with the other guy. I had a chick sitting next to me who wanted to fool around, but I had no idea what the hell she was talking about. So we thumb-wrestled for a while until she started making her moves on me.

Anyway, we were gone all day. We went to White City Park to hang out and stopped to get a soda. Normally at school, lunch was only fifty cents, but my parents always gave us a dollar every day. My dad would leave the bills on the kitchen counter for us before he left for work. Since we saved the extra, we had plenty left over for our little excursion. I had a blast.

When it was time to go back, we acted like everything was good. Still, I had a nagging suspicion as we walked through the churchyard on the way home. "Man, I think we got caught," I told John.

And he was like, "Nah, we're good."

But as we made our way through the fence in our backyard, we saw our mom sitting at the kitchen table through the glass doors. She had *the look* on her face, and her foot was tapping on the floor. I could tell how aggravated she was because she was smoking a cigarette; as she drew in, I could see the red cherry light up before she blew it out.

John opened the sliding glass door and stepped in. I walked in right behind him.

"How was school today?" she asked in a tone that told us everything we needed to know.

I thought, *Oh, shit, we're busted.*

Undeterred, John answered, "It was great."

"You weren't *at* school – get your fuckin' asses in the car!" she screamed.

So we had to get in the car and go back to school, where we got detention. My mom, of course, read us the riot act, and when we got back home, we got our asses beat. It was crazy. I never really skipped classes after that…with John. *I* figured out how to do it better. John ruined me because, after our little escapade, I constantly skipped school and never really went back again. I blew off 40 days in a nine-week period, which is

45 days, and still passed all my tests. We'd go in, sign in, and then leave.

As I mentioned, sometimes I'd cut school to surf; other times, I'd get up at 4 a.m. to surf before school. We learned how to do it on a board that didn't have any fiberglass on it; it was just the foam. And it peeled your skin off, like sandpaper. We didn't know any better. The board would just go all over the place because it had no fin. So you'd just get on it and try and ride it. The next time you got in the water with that rash, it would burn so bad, it would almost rub your titties off. But once I learned how to surf well, it became one of my favorite things to do. While you're out on the water, it's just you and the ocean. It gives you clarity and peace because no one is calling you on your cell phone or instructing you where to go for your next call. At the same time, you're vulnerable to Mother Nature and her creatures.

In terms of cutting class, I remember a funny story involving my friend Donny. He wanted to skip school with his girlfriend, Wanda, and asked if I could cover for him since we had almost all of the same classes. Of course, I said, "yes." When his mom found out, she brought him back to school. She was so mad at him when she turned to go out through the glass door, she walked right into the big wall of glass. Donny told me you could hear her glasses hit with her face. Then she turned around and whipped his ass again.

Somewhere around this time period, my little brother told me he was coming home from high school one day when he saw Donny running out the front door, with his mom chasing him down the street with a mini-griddle to beat his ass. The cord was waving in the air as she pursued. So funny. We just raised hell. High school was so much fun.

THE BLACK SHEEP (EVENTUALLY) MAKES GOOD

As we got older, the three brothers all started going our own way. Peter was doing really well and had a great career at Winn-Dixie. My brother John had a growing career at McDonald's. And there I was, the middle one, who basically had nothing. I was quitting and working everywhere I could possibly work. I'd quit and go somewhere else; quit and go somewhere else. That was my pattern. I never kept a job. So the entire time I was going through fire standards, my dad said if I wanted to go to college, which is fire school, he would pay for it. And he did.

Neither one of my parents thought I was going to finish. Well, I finished. Then, they didn't think I was going to pass. I passed.

After graduating, I went through an interview process with multiple departments. Donny got hired right away with Saint Lucie County. It took me almost two years to get hired. We had been the first night class the Indian River Community College (IRCC) ever put together. Chiefs, lieutenants, and captains all taught us in a tough program that ran Monday through Thursday from 5:00 – 10:00 p.m. and all day Saturday. It was rigorous. Back then we had to have 340 hours total. We learned about equipment, apparatus, ropes, bunker gear, and air packs. They taught us everything we needed to know about being a fireman. At the end of the six months, you take a state test, known as *The Big Three*. You're shaking while you do ladders, air pack, and hose. After that, you pass your state exam with a minimum requirement.

It's written and practical. You pass the written, take the practical; pass the practical, and receive a certificate from the State Fire Marshall. Then you're OK to go out and try to get a job, which we did.

Two years later, I still wasn't hired. Since the law in Florida states that if you're not hired within two years, your certificate of compliance expires, I had to get a job. And I was trying everywhere, but nobody would hire me. It's incredibly competitive. I even went all the way to Punta Gorda on the Gulf Coast and tested. I missed the test date by a day because of mail. Back then, there was no email, and I never got the notice in time via the regular mail. I got the letter a day late. Even though I showed up for the test like I was supposed to, they'd already tested the day before. But they were nice enough to go ahead and test me anyway.

Afterward, the Chief sat me down and said, "Son, you did great; better than everybody else. But you're not from here. So I can't hire you. I have somebody who lives here, and it would really look bad for me to hire an outsider when I have a kid right here."

"OK," I said.

The irony is, once I got hired with Brevard, I was offered jobs everywhere else. Even more ironic? As a landscaper, I'd made $17,000 per year; when I got hired by the Brevard County Fire Department, I made $15,600 per year. Yes, I took a significant pay cut. I'd also taken on a much more serious job, but I had no clue about that.

I remember five of us had an eight-week orientation with the department, but I wasn't wearing my uniform. At the time, I was still doing air-conditioning and wearing my air-conditioning pants and a blue shirt that made me look like a fireman. They put me at Station 23 on Merritt Island, which is now 41.

By the time I was five years in, my dad actually started taking notice. "Hey, he might actually do this," he informed my mother, who shared his enthusiasm. That Christmas, they bought me a gold charm in the likeness of the fire department symbol, which told me they approved of my new career. And I wore it forever.

One day, while I was working with Joe M., my dad stopped by the station to see me. While the three of us were talking, we got a call for a gas leak in a garage, where a car was leaking gasoline. Immediately, Joe and I got in the engine and went, with my dad following in his car.

When we pulled up and headed onto the scene, my dad walked into the garage where were standing.

And Joe was like, "Spike, man, you gotta tell him."

So I had to walk back and catch my father before he came back in because he was trying to help. I explained, "Dad, this is what I do. I love you. But you can't help me."

Seeing the disappointment on his face, I teared up. "Just go back to the station; I'll be there in a minute," I promised.

"OK."

After I fixed the leak, I returned to the station to find him waiting for me. "Dad, I love you, but you can't help me," I explained again.

"No, no, no, I got it. It's just, this is the first time I've ever seen you go to work. I'm pretty proud of you," he declared.

A couple of years later when we had the firestorms in the early 90s, my parents drove up to visit me at the station. Whenever they came by, they always brought a bunch of cheeseburgers for the crew and me. Covered with soot, I had just gotten back after being out all day. I was absolutely filthy; still wearing my bunker pants, which had been yellow when I'd started my shift, but were now black. I was soaking wet. And now I had to try to get the truck back in service somehow in the parking lot.

Dad called out, "You alright, kid?"

"I'm fine. It was just a long day," I answered. It was summertime, and the heat was excruciating. But it was great to see them.

Since my dad never really understood what I did, I bought him the book, *The Gun and Knife Club: Scenes from an Emergency Room*$_2$. It's about 24 hours in a Denver E.R. Although not specifically about firemen, it gives people an idea of what we do, and how fast things happen. It was the only book I could find that explained what I did for a living. On the inside cover, I wrote a brief summary for him,

"On each call, and they're all different, you can see a life taken, and one born, within minutes. It's not easy, because the way you guys raised me, I leave a little piece of me on every one. They give us this gear, and it protects us on the outside. But I'm everything I am now because of you. And I'm glad you're proud of me."

As the black sheep of the family, I had worked too many different jobs to count. But to see my father gloat when he told people what I did filled me with a sense of accomplishment. Often, he'd go around to other fire stations in St. Lucie County to get his blood pressure taken and tell them his son was a lieutenant up in Brevard. It felt indescribably good to have earned his respect and approval.

BROTHERLY STRIFE, DIVORCE, AND STOLEN IDENTITY: HOW THE FIRE DEPARTMENT BECAME MY FAMILY

It happened during a period of difficult times for all three Schneider brothers: Peter, John, and me. Peter and John had both fallen into a darker side, characterized by drug abuse. Peter became addicted, which cost him his job at Winn-Dixie, along with a great girl. Aside from the wonderful lady he's seeing now, she was probably the best thing that ever happened to him.

Although John and I were both going through divorces, I was the only one who had a decent job and a driver's license. Because John didn't pay his child support, his license was suspended, while

Peter lost his because of drugs. Each of them had gotten pulled over on different occasions, and both times, they pretended to be me by using my name. Consequently, I got a Failure to Appear in one county; then a Failure to Appear in another. When I got suspended from work, I had to go and fix it.

Two different times – three months apart.

Later on, a District Chief called me at work and said, "You gotta go home."

"What happened?"

"Your license is suspended."

I got charged with Failure to Appear, Felony, Misdemeanor, Loitering, Prowling, and Petty Theft. I had to take time off, drive to the west coast, and sit in a judge's chambers until told to go and get fingerprinted. Afterward, I went back to the judge's chambers to sit with the deputy who had pulled my little brother over. He told the judge, "That's definitely not him." I had to get a Nolle Prosequi, which is a formal notice of abandonment by a Plaintiff or a Prosecutor of all or part of suit or action.

That's what my brothers did to me – more than just twice, but several times. It was a pattern that repeated itself over the course of five years.

Fortunately, as time has gone on, my younger brother and I have worked out our differences. He's doing one-hundred times better and is now an on-air radio personality. He's doing fantastic. And I'm happy for him. I mean, I wasn't perfect when I was growing up, either. I didn't do drugs, but I was terrible with money. Anybody can tell you that. I once wrote a check for a dollar that bounced. Not kidding; it's true. I was coming back from Daytona, and I needed gas in the motorcycle – just a dollar's worth. I asked this guy, "Hey, can you give me a dollar?" He gave me a dollar, and I wrote him a check, which bounced later on. My fault. So then I got a bad rep in the department, *Don't take a check from him*. But I deserved it.

I've always had money problems. I'm terrible with money. But if you ask me for something, I'm gonna give it to you. That's the kind of guy I am.

And I trusted my brothers.

Anyway, the reason why the fire department became my family was because my Mom and Dad supported my brothers over me. One Labor Day weekend, when I went down to see them, they said, "You need to sit down."

"Why?"

"Peter got pulled over last night, and he used your name. You've got a warrant out for your arrest."

"What happened?" I asked. So they told me.

"But it's *not* his fault," they insisted.

I walked over to the phone and dialed 911 to inform them to send a deputy to the house.

"Why are you doing that?" my mother demanded.

"Well, if they've got a warrant for me, I'm going to jail."

She started to cry.

I repeated her words, "It's *not* their fault. You guys wanna help them out, but you're selling me out. And I'm the only one who has a decent job."

"Wait a minute!" my dad yelled.

"Wait a minute, what?!" I retorted.

Finally, the deputy showed up to talk to me. "Your driver's license is suspended," he began. "I know you work for the fire department. Drive home. Get it straightened out on Monday – oh wait, Tuesday, because Monday's a holiday. There's no warrant out; you're good."

By now, my mom was sobbing, and my dad was agitated.

I waited at the house for Peter to come back. As I sat in the recliner, I watched the front door, which was made of nice, thick, hard wood.

When he walked in, he was holding onto the door knob since he'd seen my car.

"Hey!" he greeted me.

"Hey!"

"What's up?"

"I don't know; what's up?"

"We cool?"

"For now."

He let go of the doorknob and took a step inside. By then, I was already in his face and punched him in the nose. His head hit the door, and when he slid down, I grabbed him by the shirt because he was almost unconscious. Then my parents tried to intervene, and I warned them if they got any closer I was going to punch them.

"You're making a mess," Mom said.

So I opened the door and dragged him out to the front yard, where I punched him again. "I'm gonna miss three days' worth of work and it's going to cost me $250. And I'm gonna miss my overtime because it's my high cycle. You owe me the money," I informed him.

While he was still rolling around on the lawn, I went into the house, grabbed a towel, wrapped ice in it, walked back out, and put it on his bloody face. Then I headed back in, stormed into his room, and took everything he had – his TV, VCR, anything of value.

"You got two weeks," I declared as I strode past him. "Get my money." And I left.

After this incident, I didn't talk to my parents for almost four years.

The fire department became my family because no matter what happened in my life; no matter what I did or somebody else did, I always got to go to work. When I left after 28 ½ years, it was like walking out on my family.

SO YOU WANT TO BE A FIREMAN?

"A hero is no braver than an ordinary man, but he is braver five minutes longer."
– Ralph Waldo Emerson

If you want to be a fireman, understand it's not about the fires. Yeah, you'll have a few. You'll have some good ones, and you'll have some bad ones. You'll get burned. It happens. But my first six months on the job, we didn't run one fire, even though I was stationed at one of the busiest houses in the county.

My first call was a fatality. I had just gotten into work when a pager came in, and my lieutenant said, "We got a call. You're driving," and pointed to me. I'd never driven a firetruck.

"Get in the truck," he ordered.

I started to put on my bunker pants, and he yelled, "No, no, no! It's not a fire call; it's a medic call. You don't need it." So I threw them in the bay. You're supposed to throw them in the truck, but I didn't know that at the time.

There were three of us on board: my lieutenant, a guy named Wayne, and me. We were headed to Diana Shores Boulevard. When I got in the truck, my lieutenant told me, "Turn the batteries on."

I looked around for batteries but had no idea what I was

looking for. Because I turned the key and nothing happened. He reached over and turned the battery with two clicks, then turned the key and started the engine. As we headed toward the scene, Wayne, who was riding tailboard, decided to mess with me. He was swinging his legs all around on the back of the truck; you know, just having a good time. Finally, we pulled up in front of the house. I went to put the truck in park but there was no park.

"Put it in neutral, put it in neutral," my lieutenant demanded.

I pulled the brake and shut the truck off. Then he yelled, "Don't shut the truck off!"

Obediently, I started it back up and got out. Now I'm looking around because everybody's gone; I don't know what house I'm supposed to go to.

Noticing the delay, my lieutenant opened the front door and exclaimed, "Over here!"

I quickly got into the house, where I saw them working on an older woman, who was probably in her 80s or 90s. Wayne started CPR and asked me to do compressions. As I did as he instructed, my hand was actually touching her boob. And he was like, "Quit feeling her up man!"

Wayne messed with me the whole time. We did CPR, but she didn't make it.

This particular call didn't affect me because I was new. I was like, *Okay, okay, I got it.* I never really thought about it because I didn't have the opportunity. At this point, I was still in training, and I had to clean the station and four trucks, which left little time for contemplation. I had a checklist for each truck: go through every compartment to make sure it contains what it's supposed to; pull the O_2 out and make sure that's full; check the oil and the water; examine the water tank and make sure the nozzles are right; wash it; clean it; and move on to the next one.

It was an ongoing process. Because each shift likes something a little different on the engine, each shift we'd move stuff around and the next shift would then move it to wherever they liked it. Not a big deal.

Then came my first traumatic call. We were up at Venetian Way getting paychecks because we delivered the checks on Merritt Island. We took them to Stations 43 (21 at the time) and 42. While on the way, we got a call to respond to Atlantic Nautilus for a gunshot wound to the face. We responded, along with 43, and got there as fast as we could. By the time I walked around the front, they had already removed the lady from the vehicle. As I looked at the car, I could see body fat and the explosion of her face all over the side of the windshield, which was splattered with blood. When I got to her, she was laying on her right side (if memory serves correctly) and her arm was flat because she'd shielded her face with it. The bullet was a hollow point; it had shredded part of her arm and hit her in the face, essentially peeling it off.

You know when you open a box of pizza and it lifts off the cheese? Well, her face looked like a piece of pizza with the cheese taken off. And her lips and other facial features were gone. She had licked her teeth…and that froze me right there. I shook like a leaf and felt as if I would vomit. But then I had to go and get parts of her face out of the car, along with Joe M. We put whatever we could salvage in the back of the rig with us, in case they could do something reconstructive.

When we got in the truck to drive back to the station, I was still shaking and trying to figure out if this was what I wanted to do with the rest of my life. Was being a fireman truly what I wanted for my career? Like a graphic scene out of a horror movie, this incident rattled me, but somehow I got through it and stayed in for another 29 years.

How did I learn how to deal with it?

You don't. If you've got a good crew, when you get back they'll make jokes. Traumatic calls are not something firemen get used to. You don't get *used* to it. You get *cold* to it. And sadly, you get cold to other things. I remember when my daughter was young, and I'd been in it about ten years. Accidentally, I shut her fingers in the car door and then yelled at her, "Just open the door!"

When I went around to get her hand out, I was like, "There's nothing wrong with it." I blew it off. "I've seen worse, not a big deal, kiddo." Then I caught myself and thought, *What the hell am I doing?*

Here's how I look at everything now: when you get in fire school, they teach you how to fight fires, use the equipment, and drive the truck. They give you the bunker gear. When I got hired and put that suit on, it was like nothing could get to me.

But what I quickly learned after a couple of years is that the suit of armor has holes in it.

And it's not only firemen; cops have it just as bad as we do. There's no real outlet. Yes, there are people you can call who will come and sit with you to discuss the horrific scene you've just dealt with. Outside of that, there's an Employee Assistance Program, which is good. You get four- to- six free sessions before it comes out of your insurance. But once you get out of the department, there is no assistance. When soldiers come home, they have PTSD. They go away to war to face its atrocities and then they come home. I'm not saying we're anything like what they do; we're not. They fight the wars away; we fight the ones here. But when they leave where they've served to come home, they come *home.*

We don't leave the warzone. We're in it 24/7. And you can say it's not a war zone but look at what's happening these days.

There's multiple shootings, there's violent crimes. All of this is going on constantly; it *is* a warzone. It's a warzone for cops, it's a warzone for fire. And when we leave there, we don't get to come home. We *go* home, but we're still in the zone. We don't get to leave. And for us to debrief, there's no real way to do that other than walking through our own front door and leaving it behind. I always thought of my home as my castle. This is where I come to be safe. Up until recently, I'd lost that. I had it and lost it, but now I'm starting to rebuild my castle. And that's the way it should be.

I'm not going to lie; being a fireman is a difficult job. The Fire Department nowadays is not what it used to be. We don't sit around and play checkers. You're training 12-14 hours a day; you don't sit down much. If you're not training physically, you've got your nose in a book. Because everybody wants you to do everything: you're a doctor; you're a lawyer; you're a psychiatrist; you're a pharmacist; you're a best buddy; you're a shoulder to cry on…you're all these things to everybody. And people don't realize what we really do.

I mean, once we even got yelled at for going to get food in the fire truck.

"You're burning fuel!" they reprimanded us.

"Well, you're right. I am. But I was already out."

It's pointless to bring in food from home. It gets ruined because we don't have time to eat. Do you have any idea how many meals we cook that we end up throwing away? You don't have the time.

And the worst thing a private citizen can say to a fireman or a cop is, "I pay your salary." Because if you think about it, they're paying their own salary. We're taxpayers, too. Don't come up to a fireman and tell him, "I pay your salary."

You *don't* pay my salary. *I* pay my salary.

Over the years, countless people have said this to me, and I have always responded, "No, I pay my salary. As a matter of fact, this guy over here in the blue shirt pays my salary. This other guy pays my salary. You know what? I pay their salaries. We're all taxpayers."

But as I said, the Fire Department is not what it used to be. It will break you down. Either it'll break you down on the front half and leave you miserable in the last half, or when you leave in the last half, it'll come back – all of the emotions will wreak havoc on your mind and soul. For instance, I once ran a call where the lady had just had twins. She woke up one morning when the babies were about two weeks old. As we rushed in through the front door, I remember the husband saying she got up, walked out into the living room, and just passed out. The second we got there, he told us she was a code; she was not breathing.

We started working her. There we were, trying to bring someone back to life who had just given birth to two. And her husband was crying in front of us, asking us what he has to do: "What am I gonna do with my kids? What am I gonna do? I can't go with you. I have my babies. What am I gonna do?"

He knew what was going on, I gathered because he sensed what we were doing was not good.

As a fireman, I'm sitting there and I'm working, doing all of the things I'm supposed to do. But I'm hearing this. And you're supposed to keep your composure. Keep it together. And we are, you know, we're doing our job, especially knowing she'd just had twin babies two weeks ago.

But when you leave the call, you never really leave.

Kids are the worst calls you could ever handle. You don't ever want to run kids. But a mom who just had twins? That's pretty bad too. Even today when I smell something, it'll take me back to a particular call. You know, I remember the entire scene in vivid detail.

Whenever we ran traumatic calls or something particularly bad, and we thought someone was freaked out about it, we'd come together, just a small group of us, to discuss it. But the memory never goes away. It's like if you smell something, it'll take you right back to where you were. Like I said, people in the military get to leave and come home; but I drive down State Road 520, and I see the accident with the eight kids in it. I hit a section of Interstate 95, and I think of the violent crash scene.

The hardest part about what we do is forgetting about what we've done. And that doesn't happen. You'll never forget.

How does it affect me in my life outside of work?

I would say, in a good way…and a bad way. On the positive side, I appreciate the people I love. I appreciate the fact I get to wake up in the morning. I appreciated the fact that I was going to work with some of the best people in Brevard County, and in the world, as far as I'm concerned. You find that you are grateful for every second of every minute of every hour of every day. Whether you're with a loved one or someone who's just there with you in that moment, you appreciate them even more, because you don't know what's coming up. On the bad side, we get to run nursing home calls and see where we're going to end up once we reach a certain age. We know how people are going to treat us when we do.

There's a ton of weight on firemen and cops these days, but nobody thinks about what happens afterward. And that's where the cities and counties need to start doing better; preparing for when their boys retire. Support for PTSD[3] would be a great start. If retired firemen and cops had resources – a network of professionals willing to donate their services, a support group, or some kind of compensation for one-on-one treatment or counseling, it would improve the quality of their lives. Because the job affects you, period. In every way, shape, and form including your personal relationships, ability to communicate, and willingness to trust. For years, I built a protective wall around me. It's just an indescribably rough life.

If you want to be a fireman, understand that a fireman's role is not the same anymore. It's not as if you just sit in the station and wait for a call. You literally are a servant to everybody. *Everybody.* You never stop being a fireman. I'm retired, and I never stop. If somebody needs help, I'm there. That's what a fireman is.

Do I think we are heroes? No. Not one damn person. But there are heroes around every day. My hero? My hero was my wife or my girlfriend; whoever had to keep my house running while I was gone. That's my hero.

And if you're gone for 24 hours, your wife should be your hero, especially if she's taking care of your kids. Because she's mom, she's dad. She's taking your kids to school and soccer practice; she's making sure they're bathed and fed for 24 hours while you're gone. That's a hero. Because she makes life function every day. With or without you, those necessary activities go on.

When we go away to take care of brush fires, we can be gone two weeks, two days, a few hours…there's no telling. But guess who's running the house? That's a hero.

I was blessed to have worked with some of the finest. My good, decent co-workers understood the value of humor and never missed an opportunity to express it. Case in point: six months into my career, I was working OT. While I was on a call with another fireman, we ended up somewhere we weren't supposed to be in terms of the fire, and it melted my hair. When we were done, I went and got it cut. I came back two shifts later with short hair that was sticking straight up, so they starting calling me Spike. Two days after that, when I came back to work, I found an old, rusty, concrete nail with maroon shag carpeting glued on top of it, sitting on my locker. Scribbled in permanent marked was the name, "Spike." I've had the nickname ever since.

During the Mothers' Day brushfires on May 14, 2008, I was working with a guy named Dewey, who was literally driving the fire truck and talking to his wife, telling her she looked good... while we were in the middle of a fire. That was hilarious. We had flames on both sides of the road, we were coming over the top of the truck, I was riding shotgun, and I could hear him. I was like, "Get off the phone!" Then I heard him say, "I gotta go; you look great, I thought that dress was nice. Alright, bye!"

Over fifteen years ago, a man whom I'll refer to as Chief M. developed an infection that killed him. His death inspired the formation of the Honor Guard, and I am proud to say I am one of the founding members. We wear Marine-cut uniforms for funerals and ceremonies.

Then there was the young fire medic who died of leukemia. He'd worked with us at Station 43, and I remember the day he called Lieutenant K.M. to tell him he had rectal bleeding. His lieutenant advised him to go to the doctor immediately. After he was diagnosed, everybody shaved their heads in solidarity because he was losing his hair. I am ashamed to say I did not because I've got an ugly head. But that's not an excuse. I don't think Lieutenant K.M. ever got over the loss.

In my 30 years of service, we lost several people due to natural causes. Each one of them is missed, talked about, and thought about in one way, shape, or form on a daily basis. The ones who made you laugh, the ones who were great medics, the ones who were exceptional leaders, the best firefighters you've ever had… not one of them can ever be replaced.

So yes, these are quality people. And the only reason I went to work, other than a paycheck, although in Brevard County you don't get paid that much. You could leave here and go to another department and make almost double what we're making.

Why?

Because this county doesn't want to raise your taxes. These first responders stay here not because of the wages, but because they don't want to go anywhere else. They're committed to this county, this department, and these citizens. They are loyal, upstanding public servants. The best. For three decades, we were asked to do more with less in Brevard County. And we have.

And they'll continue to ask us to do that because we will.

You may not know this, but your average firefighter has an AA or an AS Degree. Probably one-quarter have a Master's Degree but still they refuse to go anywhere else. They stay here and do the job they love. And it's not really the job; it's the people they work with.

Let me tell you, I would literally would go to hell and back with my brothers and sisters if I had to. In fact, I probably have a few times.

HORROR ON THE HIGHWAY

"You're safer in the race car than you are
in cars going to and from the track."
– Mario Andretti

As I mentioned, it's not about the fires. Some of the worst calls I've ever had to deal with involve automobile accidents, like the one that occurred sometime between two and three a.m. on State Road 528 when I was working at Station 41. It was a beautiful, clear night as I drove to the scene. When we rolled up, we saw a pick-up truck on its roof and an old Nova probably about 75 feet behind it. Both vehicles had obvious damage, but the driver of the Nova was still sitting in the car. The cops were already there. We stopped the truck at the bottom of the incline to block traffic.

My lieutenant asked me to go check on the driver of the upside-down pickup truck, which appeared to be a Toyota. As I approached, I noticed he was missing parts of his skull, and his head was hanging out the back of the window. When I reached in to check, he had no pulse. He was definitely expired.

I walked back toward my lieutenant and looked down at the road, where I determined that the impact had hit the truck so hard, it bent the leaf springs down, like hooks. There was a trail that clearly indicated where parts of the guy's head had slammed into the highway each time: blood, then a little further, a piece of skin with hair on it. The crash had flipped the truck and forced his head out the window, causing it to make violent contact with the road repeatedly. "He's dead," I announced to my lieutenant.

And the driver of the Nova was fine…and drunk.

We sat there while the cops did their investigation, conducted the DUI procedure, and arrested him. Afterward, one of the deputies, who'd made the phone call to the family, came up to us and announced, "His sister is getting married tomorrow. He was out catching shrimp for the wedding."

While we sat in somber silence in the truck at the bottom of the hill, it started to rain. *But there were no clouds.* And as I watched I thought, *What the fuck?* Then I gazed up at the pickup truck at the crest and saw blood mixed with rain hitting the cracks in the bridge.

My lieutenant, who wasn't a very religious man, couldn't have said it any better: "I guess God's claiming this one tonight."

And I just thought, *Wow. Tears of God.*

Then we had to remove the body with the coroner out there. The victim wasn't very old; still in his 20s. Three hours had passed, and I remember thinking that somebody – his wife, his girlfriend, his mother – had been wondering where he was before she received that terrible call. Thanks to someone else's irresponsibility, a young man's life ended. Yes, this one hit me hard.

By the way, whenever there's a fatality in an accident, the reason it takes so long to clear is because there has to be a homicide investigation. The victim must be identified, the next of kin notified, and the body removed.

BURNING UP ON 528

Years ago, there was a toll plaza on State Road 528 that always got backed up at a certain time, which meant you just knew there was high probability of getting a call. One, in particular, stands out in my mind. We responded and went running up to 528, where one of the cars was on fire. The passengers had just been pulled out – a mom and dad in front, and a daughter in the back who appeared to be around eleven or twelve. I went over to help the young girl, but her pupils weren't even visible; they were rolled back in her head. Although she wasn't burned, she was guppy breathing, or to put it in medical terms, engaging in agonal breathing.$_3$ Once I called the medics, they got there pretty quick. One started working on the daughter and told me to go help with the other one.

In the background I heard the dad yelling, "It burns, it burns!"

I went over and held his head, which had portions of the roof stuck on it because the car had melted inside. He was wearing one of those nylon football jerseys that had succumbed to the heat and stuck to his shoulders. His crimson face was brutally blistered, and he was screaming in agony. I tried as hard as I could to keep his crunchy head still when we put him on the backboard. Then because Rescue needed a driver I had to drive the rig all the way to Wuesthoff Hospital with the two patients, where we unloaded them and brought them to the E.R. Afterward, I was stuck cleaning the rig, but as I was doing it, another Rescue there got called for another accident on 528. So I jumped on that Rescue to get back out there with my lieutenant. It turned out to be a pretty bad accident because the first one we'd just handled ended up causing the second one. While they were still cleaning up from that one, the backed-up traffic created another collision.

That day, I didn't get back to the station until about two

or three in the afternoon. The two accidents resulted in a crazy domino effect in which I left the station with my crew at 9:00 a.m. and drove the rig to the hospital twice. And while on the rig we ran more calls on the way back.

PICKUP OUT OF CONTROL

I once ran a call where the driver lost control and flipped his pickup on the way to his job at UPS. Arriving on-scene, we saw that Engine 40 was just sitting there because its crew didn't want to cut the guy out. "It's pretty disgusting," they explained. Taking on the responsibility, I moved toward the vehicle, and as I got close, I noticed it was a small-sized pickup on its roof. While I prepared to do the extrication, I heard somebody screaming. With the Jaws[4] in hand, I approached on the driver's side, where his head was hanging out the back window. Due to the impact of the pavement, it had a certain flatness to it; he was resting in a halo of blood with brain matter oozing out.

As I worked to get him out, a car pulled up, even though the deputy had blocked the road: it was his wife, screaming at the top of her lungs. There I was, doing my best to cut him out and I could hear her shrieks of pain and anguish. Then the other two guys started to break down because it was killing them, too. All the while, I struggled to extricate him in the best possible way so we could cover him with a sheet. But it just kept sliding off. By now, she was on her knees, sobbing. And all we could do was walk up to her and say, "We did everything we could." Be that as it may, it doesn't take away her pain.

After a horrific call like this, I would go back to the station and mentally replay it in an endless loop.

ACCIDENT AT SHIFT CHANGE

It happened one morning when I was on beach shift, preparing to go home. We'd completed our station duties and were in the process of relaying information (known as a "pass-down") to the next shift when the call came in: "Engine 47, Rescue 47, respond to I-95, mile-marker 191 for MVC (motor vehicle crash) with multiple patients."

As we watched C shift pull away, all eight of us on B shift thought, *this could be a good one.* Then we heard the size-up (assessment) of the first arriving unit: multiple patients ejected, three trauma alerts, two trauma codes, and three Class-3's (walking wounded).

We grabbed our gear, jumped into our personal vehicles, and drove to the scene to assist. It was so bad, there was a lieutenant for every two patients and three medics for every patient. As I stepped out, I looked at one of the female lieutenants who was running the scene and announced, "I'll take this one." She nodded her assent before asking for more units.

My patient, one of the trauma alerts, had multiple facial fractures and some brain matter loss. Two medics asked for the crike to intubate. As one got up to grab a tube, I noticed his brown bunker gear was completely red, having been fully saturated with the blood of the victim. Thankfully, the crike was successful and as more Rescues arrived and helicopters landed, I surveyed the scene for others. I directed somebody to assist someone else with the Class 3's because we had enough people on-scene.

Once we completed the work, assured that the on-duty shift could handle the rest, I went back to the station, where I ordered replacement gear for *thirteen* people. That's how horrific the damage had been.

HEAD-ON COLLISION ON STATE ROAD 3

One day while working at Station 62, one of our favorite deputies stopped by in civilian clothes. We'd been chit-chatting in the living room when a call came in for an MVC on State Road 3 (South Tropical Trail), north of Pineda Causeway, at around 11 a.m. As we were getting on the truck, the deputy asked, "Hey, can I go? I don't really get to go on anything good."

"OK, but this is probably gonna be bullshit," I told him. From my experience, most of these calls involved minor fender benders or a light bump or scratch. Since it was a low-speed road, I wasn't expecting it to be serious.

With the deputy on-board, we headed north on South Tropical, where we encountered severe traffic congestion before coming upon the accident. Once we arrived on-scene, we found two older vehicles: A Chevy Blazer and a K Car, which had heavy damage to its the front end. From the K Car, a victim hung out of the passenger side door, covered in blood from head to toe, with his arm nearly touching the ground, where a crimson puddle had already formed. With an audience of about 15-20 watching, the deputy started chest compressions on him.

With only three people on my Engine and two on my Rescue, before I even got out of the truck, I told them we had a trauma code. As I stepped out, I advised one of my guys to grab the Hurst Tool because we were going to need extrication. Meanwhile, my medic on the other Engine rushed over to help the patient in the K Car.

When I got to the second vehicle, I found one of the passengers with a right ankle compounded through his skin; his bone was protruding through and resting on the dirt on the floor while his right wrist had a forked-wrist fracture. When he saw me, he told me he was OK and that he wasn't in any pain. I got on the radio, giving size-ups and requesting more units before walking around to the driver's side of the K Car, where the patient barely had a pulse rate. Her leg, from about mid-shaft to the shin to up over the knee, was completely avulsed, meaning the skin had been pulled back. So I was looking directly at her bone.

While my two medics from the Rescue worked on the male patient, I turned to my medic who was on the Engine and asked, "What do you got?"

"Well…he's got a rate of about 30 – "

"Is he fucking dead or alive; what do you got?" I interrupted.

"He's alive."

"Work him."

I called for a helicopter and asked for additional units. By now, my driver had grabbed the two Hurst Tools and put them on the ground but had forgotten the motor. When I reached over to slide the tray out to get it, it slid back and broke my finger. It was a new motor that didn't fit with the rubber tray we usually kept in there. In order to make the new motor fit properly, we'd removed the tray. But as soon as I pulled the motor out, it just slid out of control. It had a bolt sticking out that caught my finger and broke it. The funny thing was, when I put on a rubber glove in my effort to help everybody, I couldn't put it over that finger. It flopped like a bunny ear.

I walked over to put the motor on the ground, but right before I started extrication, my portable radio went dead. When I got in the truck, I heard a district chief announce, "I'm on my way."

"How far out are you?"

"I'll be there in a few minutes."

"I'm busy. I'm really busy." Nothing more needed to be said. He understood.

"Copy that," he answered.

After that, they left me alone, because when you're working, you're working. They let me do my job. With my hand all fucked up, I began extrication, but I could barely use my finger, which was black-and- blue, red, and swollen. But we kept at it, getting the guy out who was bleeding profusely. The female victim in the other car also had a broken femur, which is the big bone in the leg. It was completely visible, white and yellow, and you could see the muscle contour around it.

As you might imagine, since it was only a two-lane road, traffic continued to back up. We had to block it entirely, so there was no way anybody could get around, nor could I get other units in. Once we finally got two of the patients loaded and on their way to the hospital, we worked on freeing the last one, the trauma code. We removed the door and roof before Arnie took hold of him to pull him out. However, someone had forgotten to cut the seatbelt. After we cut it, Arnie grabbed him again, but still couldn't get him out. Then we cut the seatbelt down low and finally freed him. By now, Arnie's front gear was saturated with blood. Worse, he herniated his abdomen as a result of working this call.

With the last patient on his way to the hospital, my entire crew was gone, leaving me there with the district chief to clean up the mess with a broken finger. As he assisted me in the effort, we joked around as we normally did under these difficult situations. In the end, within ten-to-fifteen minutes, we loaded and transported all patients off-scene while working on a two-lane road, with heavy traffic congestion.

The Five Who Lived

I awakened to a cold day room, where the TV was now playing TAPS before going off the air. Having determined that my comrades had left me sleeping alone, only to wake up with a bad crick in my neck, I pulled my tired body from the chair and headed off to the bunk. On the way, I wandered over to the back door to take a look outside and touched the glass to feel the outdoor temperature.

Yup, it's pretty damn cold out there for Florida, I thought.

With this in mind, I strolled aimlessly into the bunk room. As I climbed into bed, I heard the wind blowing outside, which eventually lulled me to sleep. At about 1:30 a.m., the shriek of the alert tone rudely interrupted our slumber. My heart was beating so loudly I could not hear the call.

"Engine 42, Engine 43, Rescue 43, and Rescue 41, respond to a vehicle accident on State Road 520, west side of the Peebles Bridge," the speaker crackled.

The normal gripes of the medics filled the room as they staggered out of their beds and into the rig. As I laid in bed, I thought, *how odd to send two rescue units and two engines to an auto accident.*

Three minutes later, another page went out for Engine 844. Then another for the Volunteer Engine 844. Now I knew it was pretty bad. At this point, I was fully awake and ready to roll, knowing we're the next to run. Suddenly, the page sounded and requested Engine 41 to respond to the incident.

As we climbed into the Engine, the bay door opened for us to go screaming into the night. My gas foot was shaking, as it tended to do when my adrenaline was pumping. The funny thing about driving an Engine is when you get a call like this, your foot involuntarily taps even as you hold it down on the accelerator. Your adrenalin's raging, and you got that nervous foot twitch going. Listening to the radio traffic on the way in, I was sure we were headed there exclusively for body recovery and warned my team to prepare themselves because it wouldn't be pretty. Just then, I turned to look at a firefighter who was still somewhat new to the department. Her face was pale, with an empty-looking stare, as if contemplating how to prepare herself to pull a body from a vehicle.

When we turned onto Merritt Avenue, I saw that the roads were clear and pushed the pedal to the floor. I glanced at my watch and noticed it was early morning – 1:45 a.m. We turned onto 520 and headed east, where the lights ahead indicated the crash scene. As we pulled up, I was instructed to set up the lights on our Engine and then report to the scene. Once I completed the task, I looked around and spotted the vehicle: it was upside-down and looked to be about an '84 or '85 Camaro, completely torn apart.

"What do you need?" I asked the lieutenant.

"Hey, we got a kid trapped in the back, and we can't get to him very well. See what you can do."

"Ok," I replied. I had a reputation for being adept with the Jaws.

I climbed down off the truck and walked toward the twisted car. On the way, I stepped over a body, noticing its young face and obvious trauma. When I turned to continue my journey to the wreck, I encountered another lifeless form. *Death was a busy man tonight, taking two young lives from this world*, I thought.

When I finally got to the passenger side of the upside-down car, the door and the hatchback were both open, with a kid hanging out of the hatchback, screaming bloody murder. Then I saw that one teenager was trapped underneath. It appeared as if the roof had been smashed flat; the hood was resting on his chest as he kicked and shrieked. Another fireman worked with the Jaws to free him. Having already sprung the passenger side door, he was trying to remove it completely. I bent over and started cutting it until it was fully off and out of the way.

Sensing his disarray and seeing the pain in his eyes, I told him to give me the Jaws and take a break. As he handed it to me and asked if I needed anything else, I requested cribbing₅ to shore up the car. I slowly lifted the car off of the kid with the tool and within 15 minutes, he was free. I didn't even get to see his face, he was packaged and loaded so fast.

Immediately, I got to work on releasing the other one who was still trapped inside. I handed the Jaws to another person on-scene and crawled into the inverted vehicle on my back. This victim was laying on his belly, hanging out of the hatch. As I looked in to determine if I could get to him, I saw the driver – still seat-belted – with a long, red syrup trailing from his head and mouth; it hit the roof and formed a puddle of blood. He also had severe trauma to the chest since his side had taken the full impact of a concrete pole smashing the door jamb of the driver's side to the hump between the two front seats. And I had to crawl past him to get to where the other patient's legs were.

Lieutenant Joe M. looked in and asked, "What do you need?"

"I need a tool."

"Which one?"

"I need the Jaws. Give me the Jaws."

I was laying on my back with the smaller pair of Jaws, which weighed approximately 60 pounds, in one hand, holding my hand between my chest and the tool. I lifted it up to where I could get the tips of it in between the hump and the door jamb, but I had to use it a little at a time to pry it open carefully. I had to try to bend something out, close it, reinsert it, and open it.

Painstakingly, I had to peel the vehicle away from the trapped victim because he couldn't get out. But in order to do so, I had to lay on his legs a little bit, which I knew was hurting him. All he could do was scream the entire time.

On top of his ear-piercing sounds, the smell of alcohol and blood permeated the interior of the Camaro and assaulted my senses as I tried to focus on his legs. He'd been sitting directly behind the driver, and the sheer force of the impact had pinned his feet, from about the ankles, between the door jamb and the hump. He had a broken femur and, I had no doubt, broken ankles and legs.

"Just shut up, I'm trying to get you out!" I yelled at him.

As laid on my back looking around, the car flooded with blood. My flashlight fell into it, and as I watched, its yellow light turn crimson. My lieutenant asked me what I needed, and I requested the bigger set of Jaws. But as I tried to lift it to the metal wrapped around his legs, it was too heavy. I needed another pair of hands to help, but there was no room. I raised the tool to the area again, while another fireman worked the open-and-close valve. Slowly, we began to make headway, but it was a long, torturous process.

Although we were starting to tire out, we hung in there. When our lieutenant wanted to know how long it would be until we freed him, I yelled back at least another 25 minutes. Suddenly, I heard the sounds of a helicopter in the distance. I backed out of the vehicle and told my lieutenant we could use the Ram_6 to separate the rest of the metal from his body. While I waited for it, I looked around and saw all of the people standing around and watching, just waiting for the last of the living victims to be set free.

By now, the wind had picked up significantly, and the cold

air began to bite through my suit of armor. We were freezing our asses off and just wanted them to hurry up so we could go home. Medics were running around all over the place. It looked like a warzone, with bodies strewn everywhere, along with pieces of broken concrete and metal.

A tap on the shoulder snapped me back to reality. It was a volunteer, handing me the Ram. As I crawled back into the car with it, the kid I was trying to rescue began to wail about wanting to get out. All the while, I was trying my hardest to set the Ram, but it kept slipping. If it were to slip anymore, it would end up doing more harm than good.

Then a Cocoa Beach firefighter started talking to me from the hatch. We discussed a few ideas before agreeing on the only viable one: he would reach in and hold one end of the Ram while I held the other until we could get a good hold on the metal. Slowly, we began to make progress.

Then I heard the chopper setting down.

The lieutenant asked again for a time estimate, and I told him at least another 15 minutes. The chopper couldn't wait; they had another call. Finally, we freed the kid, and the medics converged to take him to transport. The urgent part of the accident was over. All that remained now were the dead bodies, with the driver still frozen in time behind the wheel.

It took another hour of cutting and prying on the metal casket to get him out. Afterward, I wandered around with another fireman to examine the damage. As we explored the area, the wind lifted the sheet from one of the bodies, so I ran over to cover it back up and looked at his face. He was heartbreakingly young.

I wondered how his parents were doing. I figured they were up pacing the floor, worrying about where he was. *Had he told anyone he loved them before he went out? Did anyone have the time to show him they cared?*

Then another gust of wind brought a chill to my spine and shook me out of my meanderings. My lieutenant instructed me to put my truck back in service and prepare to leave the scene. Everyone was silent on the ride back; what more was there to say? Each of us had performed our jobs well. At no time was anyone just standing around doing nothing. Still, it was little comfort as we returned to the station at about 5:30 a.m.

With Engine 41 in quarters, we began to talk over the call; everyone agreed it went well extrication-wise, control-wise, and in every way possible. At about 6:30 a.m., the phone rang with a request for us to return to Station 43 at 7:30 a.m. for a debriefing. Everyone involved with the call was required to attend. The debriefing, however, didn't last long; little was said before we were released.

As awful as the accident was, the morning after was almost as unpleasant. Rumors had circulated that the parents of one of the deceased was going to sue the county because of negligence. Their statement indicated that we'd all just stood around and let their children die.

My reaction?

Who are you to point a finger at me? I laid in a puddle of blood for a couple of hours, trying to free the living. Dead is dead. While I hate to see it, I will always challenge it, with no regard for my own safety. Your child isn't dead because of me. Maybe if you had been a better parent, he wouldn't have been in the car drinking with the others. Put the blame where it belongs.

The report I would have liked to have seen in Florida Today would have informed the public that there were eight kids in that Camaro. *Eight.* And five of the eight had lived because of the actions taken by the Fire Rescue Division.

Unfortunately, the only thing the newspaper reported was that three had died. Maybe if the media would (for once) make a positive statement on a negative incident, people would actually learn from them.

I can hope, anyway.

LOVE THY NEIGHBOR? ROAD RAGE, SHOOTINGS, AND INDIFFERENCE

"So whatever you wish that others would do to you,
do also to them. For this is the Law and the Prophets."
– Matthew 7:12 (English Standard Version)

This particular Memorial Day weekend was sunny and warm, with temperatures hovering around 80. It had been a fairly quiet morning – just a brush fire or two and a couple of false alarms. Then around 1 p.m. a pager sounded, "Engine 41, Rescue 43 respond to State Road 528, reference head-on collision."

"This ought to be a good one!" Fireman S. yelled as we responded.

Someone else grabbed the mic to tell dispatch we were responding and to send Engine 43 as well. With the siren blaring, we headed north into the typically heavy traffic of a holiday weekend. As we approached the ramp onto State Road 528, everything was already at a standstill. Weaving our way through the maze of cars, I saw one in the median and another in the middle of the road, but at this distance, I couldn't make out much more. I had no way of determining the extent of the damage.

With good use of the air horns and the federal siren mounted to the bumper of the Engine, we educated a few drivers on how to get out of the way. A few responded by letting us know we were number one as we passed by and acknowledged their rudeness with hearty waves.

Once we arrived on-scene, we were greeted by a highway littered with bent metal. The smaller car had come to rest on the median, with serious damage to the front and a horde of people standing around. The passenger door was open. An off-duty firefighter who happened to be there yelled for us to hurry. I ran to the rear of the Engine to grab the Jaws and the Power Unit. As I rushed over to help him, I noticed the driver's face was blue, with a thick stream of blood pouring out of his mouth as he laid on the back seat.

Rescue 43 pulled up. Dave shouted out a question about Tim's whereabouts; I called back in response that we split up because of the two cars. I set up the Jaws and started the extrication since the dashboard had been crushed down to his thighs, pinning him in. Dave intubated him and began CPR. Fireman S. helped me to hook up for the purpose of rolling the dash off of him, and as we started this process, someone else established a line and hooked him up to the monitor.

"This one is too late," he announced. "The extrication will take too long, and the patient is already dead."

I turned to look at another fireman, a guy who was new to the job and had not yet seen a death close up. He stared at the driver for a moment in silence. But I knew he had questions – questions I could not answer.

Meanwhile, Fireman M.'s patient was packaged and loaded into Rescue 43 and taken to the hospital. Then the highway patrol arrived to do their investigation. All the while, the driver's body was still in the car, with passers-by gawking at the gruesome sight. I said to S., "If they only knew how hard it is to forget what we have seen and done. We don't sit around and play checkers, and we never forget the ones we've lost."

Finally, at about 4 p.m., the trooper gave us permission to extricate the body.

The work was difficult and nasty because I had to crawl into the vehicle to unwrap the victim's foot from the brake pedal; I could feel his bones crunching and grinding through my thick gloves. I could also smell the sweet odor of alcohol and see the blood smeared all over the dash and the seats. It took an hour to remove him. When the coroner arrived and gave us the stretcher, we placed it against the car, all the way to the ground. As we started to pull the body out, I grabbed his chest, which felt like a bag full of smashed aluminum cans with the sharp edges sticking out. I looked more closely at his face and noticed his glasses were gone, but the frames were embedded in his forehead. Overcome by the sight, S. turned his head and stepped away. At last, the call ended. We were placed back in service and returned to quarters at about 6:30 p.m.

As we started cooking dinner, we discussed what we'd just dealt with and joked, "Hell, we already ruined lunch, let's see if we can make it through dinner." Just as we sat down to eat our grilled steaks, the pager sounded again: "Engine 41, Rescue 43, respond to 710 Via Havarre, reference suicide attempt."

Off we went, with our food sitting on the table untouched.

It took just three minutes to get there. As we turned the corner, we saw a young man on his knees in the front yard. When we pulled up to his house, he got up, ran to my door, and threw it open. Then he proceeded to pull me from the truck, screaming for us to hurry up.

I put my hand to his head and ordered him to get the fuck off me because we hadn't even stopped the truck yet. Finally, I pushed him away, exited the truck, and headed toward the house. Deputies arrived on the scene as the young man grabbed me again and we began to wrestle. Firemen S. and M. were busy getting the equipment and had no idea this was going on.

The deputies separated us as the other two firemen approached from around the truck. Finally, we entered the house to discover the victim laying on his back, with his head covered in blood. His wife had been doing CPR on him, and when she came up from ventilating, she spat his blood from her mouth. Her face was smeared with it, and as the tears streamed down her face, they turned red. I knelt beside the victim and began to snap the oxygen together. Fireman M. started compressions while I prayed Rescue would get there soon.

A second later, Fireman S. yelled that they'd arrived and went out to give them a hand. When I looked at the victim, I saw he was about in his mid-40s, with an entrance wound from a gun on the right side of his temple. The left side of his head was blown clean off, and part of his brain, flesh, and bone were splattered all over the wall and carpet. Then the medics walked in and told us to load and go. We put him on the stretcher and transported him to the rig.

Once inside, we started two large bore I.V.'s. The floor of the rig turned into a river of blood, sloshing back and forth like the ocean against the rocks. I exited and headed to the driver's seat since Fireman S. had never driven before. While en route, I heard all of the goings-on and got them a MED channel to the hospital. After we arrived, I jumped out and opened the rear doors to a gusher of blood and saline. I reached in to grab a hold of the stretcher and pull it out of the rig. We hurried him into the hospital to a waiting E.R. staff, but the outcome for the patient was bleak; he died soon after arrival.

Then the Engine arrived with our lieutenant behind the wheel. Once we returned to the station, we reheated the steaks we attempted to eat before. Now rubberized from the microwave, dinner was at last served. Later, as the clock struck 10 p.m., we began to wind down from the day. We completed our reports and cleaned the station for the next shift.

Then the pager sounded again. "Rescue 43 and Engine 41, respond to 375 Diana Boulevard, reference psychological problems."

That made us laugh as we ran to the truck, thinking *we* should be the ones with the psychological problems. We pulled into the neighborhood and spotted the address, along with a lady standing by the mailbox. I asked her if she needed our assistance and she told me she was having an emotional problem and was waiting for the ambulance. Rescue 43 pulled up behind us, and I gave the report to P. that she wanted a ride to the hospital. He looked at me and then back to her before telling her to climb in.

As we climbed into the Engine, the radio squawked, "Engine 41 control!" M. grabbed the mic and responded, "Engine 41, go ahead."

"Respond to 720 Bellaire Drive, reference an assault to a deputy."

"Responding."

Since we were already close to the area, we arrived within a minute or two. As I exited the truck, a naked lady ran past me, followed by a pair of deputies. M. was looking for the injured deputy but couldn't locate him. I joined in the chase for the woman after a deputy who was running by me yelled at me to give them a hand. As I passed them on foot, I asked, "Why are we chasing her? I mean, I know she's naked but…"

"She's crazy, too," came the reply.

After a good 30-minute hustle through the neighborhood, I put a full-out NFL tackle on her. I hit her in the waist and drove her to the ground like a defensive lineman sacking a quarterback. Now subdued, the deputies arrested her and brought to her own house where M. was waiting for me. He asked if I'd seen the naked lady running around the house and I replied, "Hell, she's been running naked through the neighborhood." After a short rest, the deputies took her in and thanked us for our help.

I looked at M. and inquired as to where he'd been, and he said, "I've been waiting for you."

Finally, we returned to the station. I looked at my watch and saw it was almost one a.m. I headed to the bunk to get some much-needed sleep, but it didn't last long. At two a.m. we were awakened by the screaming sound of the pager, "Engine 41, respond to 545 Roosevelt Avenue, reference garage fire!"

I staggered out of bed, ran into a groggy M., and stated, "You are bad luck." He laughed a little and told me he would never work overtime on the island again. Since the call was only about six blocks from the station, we arrived quickly. As we pulled up, we saw a black man and a black woman fist-fighting in the front yard of the duplex while a pile of garbage burned in the driveway. M. ordered me to put some water on it, then proceeded to break them up. The deputy arrived to handcuff the male and put him in the car. After I put out the fire, I kicked my way through it and realized it was clothing. In talking with the lady, M. found out that her husband had been cheating on her, so she threw him out and lit his clothes on fire.

We climbed back into the Engine, laughing about what we'd just witnessed. Once back in quarters, we agreed that the reports could wait until the morning. It felt like I had finally just gotten back to sleep when the pager sounded again. "Engine 41, Rescue 43, respond to 1155 Lucas Road, reference a shooting."

As we got into the truck, I wiped the sleep from my eyes and forced myself to focus on the road ahead. I leaned over to turn on the strobes and released the brakes. *Here we go again.* Our destination was a low-rent area for which we often got calls for assaults, gunshots, stabbings, and all kinds of violent occurrences. The place was also notorious for drug-running.

We pulled up on the scene, grabbed the trauma bag, and made our way through the crowd, the deputies having secured the area. I saw a young black man lying on his back, with his girlfriend kneeling by his side putting ice on him. When she told me he fell, I noticed she was in shock and asked her to step back and get some more ice for me; I didn't want to incite a riot by having her pulled away.

As I felt for a pulse, I could see the entrance wound to the chest. It was small – maybe about the size of a pencil eraser, with little or no blood. I discovered a pulse while M. set up the AMBU bag for ventilations. Rescue 43 pulled up as we ventilated the victim. When P. asked what we had, I gave him a report. He started a large bore I.V. and set him up on the monitor. "Shit, let's work him," he said.

M. grabbed the radio, told Control we had a trauma alert, and informed them which hospital we would be transporting him to. We loaded and went, with me driving the rig. Once at the hospital, we helped get him into the E.R., where the doctor took over after P. gave a report. As M. pulled around to pick me up, I looked out over the river and watched the sun come up; it was now 6:15 a.m. and I was wide awake. M. looked at me and said, "It has been nice working with you, but never again."

Can you blame him?

Sometimes after a night like this, it was best to just go home and get some sleep. Other times it would take two days to get my wind back. We had multiple calls during this 24-hour shift, and no two were alike. However, we had three fatalities – all from violent causes – as is the case with most. Only the lucky ones get to pass away in their sleep.

A SENSELESS SHOOTING

As I mentioned earlier, kids are the worst calls you'll ever have to make. You do not want to run kids, ever.

It was a warm and sunny afternoon during this particular shift. We'd just cleaned the station and had already dealt with a few B.S. calls. NFL football was on: The Green Bay Packers versus the Tampa Bay Buccaneers. Two of the guys were in the back studying for a test, another was doing paperwork, and I was discussing my prediction for the game with a female firefighter. Since I am a Packers fan, guess where my money was?

Around 4:30 p.m., the pager sounded, "Rescue 41, Engine 41, respond to 255 Lucas Road, Apartment 901, reference, fall."

We walked out to the Engine and climbed in while Fireman M. told Control we were responding. I reached forward, turned on the strobes, released the brakes, and got underway. As we pulled onto the road, I could see Rescue 41 right behind us. We figured this would probably be a bullshit call because the kids in that area were always calling in false alarms from the payphone out front. But once we were heading south on Courtenay, Control called us back to inform us it was a six-year-old kid. Since it was a young child, his mother was on her way home.

When we turned onto Lucas, I saw somebody standing on the corner to wave us in. I turned left into the complex with Rescue on my heels. I stopped, exited the vehicle, and noticed a swarm of people around a child lying on the grass under a tall pine. I approached and knelt on one side of him while another fireman knelt on his opposite side.

One of the other kids told me he'd been shot. I asked, "How do you know?" as we rolled him onto his back. He pointed to the window facing us and said, "That boy in there shot him."

I saw that there was blood flowing out from his mouth, and his eyes were rolled back into his head. The other fireman felt for a pulse. Nothing. A woman standing nearby screamed, "They killed my baby!"

We were surrounded by onlookers as the rest of our team arrived with the equipment. Mind you, this all went down in about a minute. One medic yelled to another to get the monitor; someone else called for the cops and began making room for us. Everyone picked up the pace while word spread throughout the devastated neighborhood that a little kid had been shot. Fireman M. took control of the crowd until the cops arrived, one fireman went to the back of the rig to start setting up, and another fireman and I began CPR.

I looked for an entrance wound, but the only visible trauma was in the mouth. My co-worker looked at me and announced, "This is a crime scene. Do not touch anything you don't have to." The crowd grew larger as Fireman M. urged us to hurry and go. One fireman grabbed the gear and hauled ass to the rig while Fireman C. and I loaded the kid onto the stretcher and transported him to the vehicle. When a deputy passed us on the way, Fireman M. yelled to him that he would need more help. As two more deputies arrived, Fireman H. stepped out of the rig and into the driver's seat to take us in.

The three of us stayed in the back of the rig with the child. One of the firemen was upset because he had a young daughter; I thought of mine as well. It wasn't easy for any of us to keep our minds focused. Here I was, with two of the best medics in the county – if not the entire state – whose knowledge and expertise shone through on every call. And all of us were fighting to maintain our composure.

I began compressions on the boy as we got underway. At the head, Fireman C. attempted to intubate$_8$, or in layman's terms, tube him. Another fireman started an I.V. in his left arm. C. announced he needed suction because the back of the child's throat was covered with blood, obstructing his view. When I heard the sound of the fluid being drained, it reminded me of the dentist: before he drills a cavity, he puts the straw into your mouth, and it makes that loud, sucking noise. Chills ran down my spine as I continued to do compressions. The blood from his mouth ran through a clear tube; it was like watching the life drain out of him.

C. tried again: this time he got it and began to intubate him. Another fireman yelled to our driver to get him a MED channel; Fireman C. grabbed the headphones and placed them on his head while the other fireman began another line on the opposite arm. The monitor didn't change; still no heartbeat. He yelled at the child to hold on while I said a silent prayer, my eyes filled with tears. This particular fireman was usually calm and not one to rattle easily, but it was clear this incident had taken a toll on all of us.

Fireman C. gave the report to the hospital as another one loaded equipment onto the stretcher in preparation for our arrival. Once we pulled in, there were nurses waiting outside. We stepped out of the rig and were ushered immediately into the trauma room, where the doctor barked out orders. Fireman C. continued to bag him, I kept up compressions, and the other Fireman C. helped transfer him to the hospital equipment.

Once the X-ray films were completed and held up to the light, you could see the path of the bullet. It had entered at the base of the skull, fragmenting and traveling upwards into the brain. It had shattered the spinal cord in a place that controls all of the involuntary muscles in charge of vital activities including breathing and heartbeat. Essentially, the child could not be saved. His life had ended.

As we began to clean up the back of the rig, Lieutenant M. pulled up in Engine 41 and told us to be prepared to go back to the home because the family was devastated. We climbed in and returned to quarters. I thought to myself, *Sad isn't it? You do the best you can do, and still nothing. The boy's mother is surely in pain. When she left him today, he was smiling and running around. And now, whenever she comes home, it will be a sad reminder of what started out as a beautiful day and ended in tragedy.*

Once back at the station, we restocked some of the engine supplies we used on the call. Everyone was quiet; it was obvious we'd all been deeply affected by what we'd just witnessed. Then we heard Rescue 41 on the radio announcing their return before the pager sounded again, "Engine 41, Rescue 41, respond to 255 Lucas Road, Apartment 502, reference chest pains."

I knew it was in regard to the young boy's death. We arrived before Rescue and made our way up the stairs to the apartment. I entered first, followed by Fireman H. Fireman M. had to stand outside because the tiny apartment was already overcrowded. When I reached the woman, I noticed she was in her late 30s. I sat beside her, took her hand, and told her how sorry I was for what happened. She could tell I was sincere by the tears in my eyes and began to weep. I slowly placed her head on my shoulder while she whispered, "My boy is gone." And there was nothing I could say or do to make her feel better.

I looked up at Fireman H. and saw that she was crying too. Then I asked the victim's mother if she wanted to go to the hospital, but through her sobs, she told me she would rather stay at home. When the two Firemen C's made their way in, we all mourned with her for a while. One of the firemen advised one of her friends to stay with her before we left to go back to the station.

Upon our return, we had little to say, but as we watched television, Fireman C. noted that the little boy was one of the kids who used to come around the station to play basketball with us. After thinking it over for a while, I couldn't remember whether he did or not. But I said to myself, *wherever he is, God bless him and goodnight.*

I responded to a call where a six-year-old child died from a gunshot wound to the head. Why? Well, the boy inside the apartment didn't like that he was playing outside his window. *What kind of society are we creating for our children? Are we teaching them that violence is the answer to everything?*

Each call an emergency worker runs inflicts irreparable damage to his or her body, mind, and soul. Yeah, there are those like Iron Mike who say, "It ain't no thing."

Bullshit.

It wears on you. You can't see it, but others can. The suit of armor begins to weather from all of the battles it has fought. If the holes are not mended, it will soon fall apart. Learn to fix what is broken; do not ignore it.

A MISSING CHILD AND A BACKYARD CANAL – A TRAGIC COMBINATION

Sometimes, tragedy strikes for no apparent reason. As with the incident I just described, when it involves babies and kids, it's even more gut-wrenching. One cool day, when I was working on Merritt Island, we got the call to respond to a missing child case. We immediately ran over to the house, and when we arrived, a little girl who was probably about seven told us, "I can't find my baby sister."

When we asked how old she was, she informed us that the child had just started walking. We frantically searched the house, but there was no trace of her. Then I noticed that the back door was open a little bit. I rushed out and saw a canal close by. *Oh shit*, I thought as I ran toward it.

And there was the baby.

I reached down, snatched her out of the water, and held her in my arms while I did compressions. When one of the medics saw me, she sprinted to the rig to begin setting everything up. I rushed through the house, still doing compressions on the toddler with partially open eyes, cool skin, and flopping arms while her seven-year-old sister watched and wondered what was going on.

Despite our best efforts, there was nothing we could do. Ironically, the medic who had acted so quickly had a daughter celebrating a birthday that day, which compounded the emotion we'd all felt. I remember that well.

Whenever we hear it's a kid, the medics – who are awesome because they know what to do – kick into action. One of them jumps in the back of the rig and starts opening up the PEDI bag and getting stuff ready. Just in case, it's open.

In the aftermath of this incident, as a boss and certainly as a lieutenant, whenever my crew arrived on-scene for a similar call I'd radio to tell them, "Stay in the rig. I'll be there in a second." Then I would go in and grab the baby or the child and bring them out. Because it is tremendous pressure when the parents, family, and everyone else are assembled, screaming and crying. It's an incredible burden on the first responders – just a huge amount of stress.

And when we're all on the scene, instead of trying to work the baby, one of us is trying to do crowd control, the other one's trying to get everything, and someone else is trying to find out "Is the baby on any medication?"

But once we get into a controlled situation in the back of the rig, we as firemen can ask questions while the medics are doing what they need to do. It allows us those few seconds or minutes we need of peace and quiet. We need to listen. We need to see what's going on.

Once I had the information, I'd come back to the rig and tell them, "This is what's happening," or "The baby has a history of this or that," for example, SIDS.[9]

Yes, you can implement a workable system to effectively deal with tragic situations involving babies and kids. But you never get used it.

AN AMBIEN "EMERGENCY"

I referenced earlier that we deal with bullshit calls too. Somebody will cut their finger and dial 911, even though there are six cars in the driveway and twelve people available to take them to the hospital. But they want to go by ambulance. I'm not kidding. I once ran a call where the guy took Ambien.

That's right: he took Ambien, a sleep-inducing medication, then called 911 because he felt drowsy. And he was sitting there with his wife (or girlfriend) and his mom. Either one of them could have taken him into the E.R., but he called us to do it because he felt drowsy. That's not a lie. I remember I stood over him and read the box: *"May cause drowsiness. Does this feel like drowsiness?"*

And I looked directly at his mom, a woman who was perfectly capable of getting behind the wheel of one of the cars in the driveway. But he had to go by ambulance. Needless to say, the ambulance in that area (47) was the only one in service, which meant Station 47 used it to transfer a B.S. call all the way down to Holmes. So if someone in the neighborhood were to have a heart attack, it would delay transport and increase the chances of death.

Because some idiot took Ambien and felt drowsy.

Somebody will call you because they have a headache, or they've had a backache for six days. There are multiple cars sitting in the driveway and someone at home who can drive them. But that's not gonna happen.

You want to know why it takes so long to be seen in the E.R.? These indifferent, inconsiderate people. Remember at the beginning when I told the story of breaking my arm, and my brother breaking both an arm and a leg, and our dad driving us to the hospital each time? We didn't dial 911; my father exercised common sense and took us in himself with his own car.

Unfortunately, common sense and consideration for one's neighbor are in short supply these days.

I remember well the church fires of the early 90s.

Back outside during the fire call on Myrtice Ave., for the 1920s building.

BRUSHES WITH DEATH: THE RAGING INFERNOS

> "I'd rather fight 100 structure fires than a wildfire. With a structure fire, you know where your flames are, but in the woods it can move anywhere; it can come right up behind you."
> -Tom Watson

Once in a while, being a fireman *is* about putting out fires. I remember a call for a structure fire on Via Havarre that I responded to with Joe M., my boss at the time. When it came in, I exclaimed, "Woo!" And Joe responded, "Yeah!" We were pretty pumped up as I got behind the wheel and drove us to the scene.

And as I mentioned, the reason why a fireman reacts with an enthusiastic *"Yeah!"* to a structure fire and a reluctant *"Bullshit!"* to an EMS call is because ninety percent of the EMS calls we deal with are crap. It'll be the Ambien guy or some other jerk who cut his hand, needs stitches and can drive himself to the hospital but insists on going by ambulance, despite the fact that there are plenty of cars and people to drive him.

But here's the thought process, *If I go by ambulance, I'll get in quicker.*

Take it from one who knows: *No, that's not how it works.*

You get walked right out to the lobby just like everybody else. It's called triage. And if you want to make a fireman or a medic's day, let us walk you out. Because we *will* walk you out. The first thing we do before we get there is radio ahead something like, "This is Rescue 43, we're en route to the facility with a Class 3 patient, stable. Got a laceration to the left hand. All his vitals are within the normal limits. He's resting comfortably on the stretcher; we'll be there in five."

The next thing we hear on the radio in response is, "Triage on their arrival."

"Copy!"

Then we walk him right through the E.R. and all the way out to the lobby. "There you go – enjoy! You got here faster."

But back to the fires.

People tend to rag on the Fire Prevention Bureau, but the truth is, they've been doing their job. Fires have decreased. The problem nowadays is that they burn hotter and more rapidly than they did years ago because of chemicals. Plastics, rubbers, vinyl, clothes, and fabrics all burn faster. Worse, the gases they emit can be fatal. Years ago, when houses were constructed of wood or concrete, you'd have a legitimate fire of wood and concrete. Today, with all the additional chemicals in the tub, the sheets, the fake wood and so on, fires burn hotter and faster.

Joe and I made our way to the scene and turned right into Villa De Palmas. From there, it was the first left. As we came around the corner, we saw a thick, black column of smoke, then caught sight of the back side of the house where we were headed, situated between two others. It was pitch black. I pulled in up front, got out, and put my air pack on while Joe grabbed the line, then we rushed to the front door. Neighbors standing around outside called out, "Nobody's in the house!"

"OK, copy!"

The blaze, which had burned down the double doors of the entrance, greeted us furiously. Since there was a straight wall directly ahead, we ducked down and went underneath the flames. But by the time we got about four or five feet in, it was too hot; we couldn't go any further. As I laid there on the hose I told Joe, "You gotta grab that other line or I'm gonna lose it!"

"OK, don't go anywhere!" he yelled.

And I was like, "OK!"

He got the second line and dragged it in. At this point Engine 43 was behind us; they came out and charged the line, while Joe and I remained inside, shooting water. And was *hot*. We got burned on our neck, in our ears, on our faces. The fire singed us badly, but we stayed with it and kept fighting.

Then 43 entered and helped us with the hose line as we advanced further and further, working efficiently to subdue the flames. It truly was a stubborn fire raging in a big house as we fought it with everything we had. After 15 minutes, my air bottle went off, giving me no choice but to head back outside for a new one. When I started to crawl out, I got stuck on something, so I grabbed onto whatever I could to pull myself across the floor. Once I got close to the door, I realized I was dragging a love seat along with me; the smoke had been so thick, I hadn't noticed when the spring took hold of my pocket. I threw it off, ran out, and yanked my bottle just as Joe came out.

We decided, "Man, let's go through the garage and approach through the laundry room." Then we pulled one of the lines out because another crew had arrived to assist. As we made our way in through the laundry room, which had a terrazzo floor, the heat was so intense that the liquid detergent had popped. So now we had soap oozing everywhere on a slippery surface. As Joe and I navigated our way in, all you could hear was our air pack bottles going, *Clank, clank, clank!* We slipped and busted our asses as we attempted to crawl across, yelling, "Holy shit!"

At last, we made it in and put the fire out. Once safely outdoors, I looked at Joe's ears, which had skin hanging off of them. He looked at me and noticed my neck had skin hanging off of it.

"You're burned!" he exclaimed.

"*You're* burned!" I replied.

Seeing us, the guys on the Rescue told us to get in the back. Joe laid on the stretcher, covered with ice packs. I sat on the tailboard and rested my head on the back of the stretcher as I held ice on it. Then our Chief rolled up and surveyed the scene. A neighbor spotted him and asked, "Are you the Chief?"

"Yes," he confirmed.

"Those first two mother fuckers," he continued, "those *first two*? Balls *this* big, I swear! They went underneath the fire, dude! They got balls *this fuckin' big*!" He gestured with his hands to emphasize his point.

I remember because I was sitting right there with the ice pack when the Chief asked, "Are your balls that big?"

Joe and I looked at each other and nodded. It was pretty funny.

FIRE IN THE OLD 1920S BUILDING

Summers in Florida can be oppressive, with high temperatures and humidity that test the mettle of even the most physically fit and healthy. That was definitely the case one 98-degree day on Merritt Island when Lieutenant B. and I got the call for a structure fire at 550 Myrtice Avenue. At the time, we ran two-man Engine companies; it was just my lieutenant and me at the Station while the other two Engine companies were off the island responding to other calls, including a gas leak. When the dispatch radioed us, we immediately jumped on the truck and raced down to the scene, not thinking too much of it.

As we turned onto Myrtice off of South Tropical, we saw a deputy waving his arms frantically in a circular motion, as if trying to make us drive faster. But we couldn't see anything until we moved past a big clump of trees. Then my lieutenant exclaimed, "There it is, there it is!"

We looked up to see thick black smoke pumping ominously out of one of the windows on the third floor. He turned to me and said, "Get up there and put that son of a bitch out."

Already wearing my bunker pants, I got out of the truck and threw my jacket and air pack on. By the time I came around from the back Rescue 43 had already pulled up with two guys on it. I tossed the hose line over my shoulder and urged, "Let's go!"

As we made our way up the stairs, we cleared each floor, busting down doors and ensuring that everyone was out of the house. Once we completed the first floor we went back around, moved up to the second floor, and cleared it. While on the second floor, I walked down the hallway unattached to air, carrying a hose line that had not yet been charged because they were still trying to get a water supply. We were the first Engine to pull up; it wasn't until after we'd entered the burning building that Engine 42 arrived and dropped the line. B. got busy making the water hook up. Since we had terrible radios back then, it was difficult to communicate.

After a while, we started to get water. As I took another step down the hall, an ember fell from the ceiling above me onto the floor right in front of me. When I looked up, I could see through the ceiling to the third floor, through the foundation of what was once the attic, but was now a raging inferno.

Holy shit.

I turned around and yelled, "Hook up, everybody, hook up!" in reference to their air packs. We got down to one last door on the right-hand side, forced it, and busted it open to discover an entire room consumed by fire. We'd later find out that this was where the blaze had originated from behind the refrigerator, in a wall socket.

Unfazed, we burst into the area like a bunch of idiots, squirting water and hootin' and hollerin' "Woo!" We thought we'd extinguished it, but as soon as I put the nozzle down – whoosh! – the fire returned with a vengeance.

Oh shit. We turned around and went back up the stairs.

The large building had been constructed of plaster and lath back in the 1920s. Small pieces of timber, about two-inches-thick and covered by plaster, ran horizontally. Later, when they renovated it into residential apartments, they put drywall over it, which held the heat well and kept the fire in check for a little while.

But when we tried to go upstairs to the third floor, it was way too hot. Everybody backed down while smoke streamed down the stairs of a huge, beautiful staircase.

"Let's try it again," I suggested. We all got down and attempted to ascend once more, with no success. The heat was too intense.

Determinedly I thought, *OK, I can do this.* I climbed on top of the banister and started breaking the posts off so I could crawl on the floor to the third level. Once I made it all the way, I reached down for someone to hand me the nozzle through the smoke and pulled it up. Damn, it was *hot* – the heat was just being funneled down that staircase. I laid on the floor as low as I could with the nozzle. At the far end of it, everything was black. I could barely make out daylight, a door at the very end. Then I opened the nozzle with the intention of cooling the area down a bit so we could get up there, but the water disappeared before it even came out. It was just gone. The unrelenting heat ate it up.

In case you didn't know, one drop of water expands sixteen-hundred times and turns to steam. Well, steam burns. Back then, we carried a fog nozzle, which converts to steam. Room temperature got so intense, I rolled down off of the stairwell on top of everybody to avoid getting cooked.

After a minute, we tried it again and, this time, made it all the way up to the third floor; my efforts to subdue the fire had been enough to make it possible. Then, second and third lines came in because Engine 44 finally got there from Cocoa, along with Engine 43. Now there were more firefighters and more hose lines getting stretched.

But since we'd been in there a good 20 minutes, everybody in our party was exhausted. One by one, they started exiting the building.

"OK," I relented.

One of the firemen met me on the third floor and announced, "Hey, let's finish busting these doors down."

In this process, as you bust the doors to enter, you search each room while a nozzle man covers the door and keeps everything in check. We worked the left side of the hallway, searching about four rooms since conditions on the floor had improved. We knew where the fire was on one side and tried to get hose lines to it.

Then we moved to the next room, where we got ourselves into deep trouble when it ignited. Over on the wall, my co-worker screamed, "We gotta get out, we gotta get out!" But there was nowhere to go; we couldn't escape.

As I looked around, I spotted a regular box fan in the window pulling air in and kicked it out of the way. Since I had a six- or seven-foot piece of rope, I looked for a way to exit. *Absolutely everything was on fire.* There was nowhere to go. In a desperate attempt to get some air, I stuck my head out the window and noticed Chief T. on the ground.

Then I laid down on top of the other fireman to keep him calm. He kept screaming he just wanted to get the hell out of there. Thinking fast, I tied the rope around the leg of a piece of furniture that was sturdy enough to hold us. The killer with this was when I leaned out of the window, the metal roof was holding the heat, which meant we would've been scrambled like eggs on top of it. But before we could even go out the window, the nozzle man came in and started knocking stuff out. Everything had turned to steam to the point where it was cooking us. We rushed out of the room on our hands and knees, crawling to the door and the nozzle man as fast as we could. Once he'd opened the nozzle, everything darkened down, but it started venting out through the window a little better. He had cooled it enough to where it was possible to get out – good thing or we both would have been well done.

We descended the stairs and made it outside as fast as we could in our tired bodies.

When I came out, Chief T. asked, "Was that you up there, looking out that window?"

"Yeah."

"Man, when I saw that all I could think was, *Good God, how can anybody be alive up there?* You had smoke and fire just blasting out over the back of your head."

"I'll be honest with you: we *were* cooked. Then the nozzle man came in."

Once outside, I just sat down on my butt, exhausted. They came up and dumped an ice cooler of water on me because my gear was still smoking. Since my co-worker had passed out, they brought him over to the tent they had set up on the ground, where they started a line and transported him to the hospital. After dragging me over, they tried to start one on me, but I refused. I just kept drinking water until I finally had to pee. Right in front of everybody, I walked over by a tree and relieved myself, not even caring.

All around me, people were dropping like flies due to the extreme temperatures; however, we still had a fire to put out. Dutifully, I put my coat and air pack back on, then talked to my lieutenant, who was still working on the Engine, pumping the hose.

"Take this two-and-a-half and go up the stairwell," he ordered. Completely worn out, now I had to drag a charged, two-and-a-half line by myself. Somehow, I managed to haul it all the way around the back of the house to the west side and up the fire escape. As I climbed higher and higher, it got hotter and hotter. With every step, I became more fatigued, but I kept going until I got to the door I'd been aiming at from inside the building. From the outside, it had a screen. Then some debris – a couple of pieces of wood – fell on me, not a total surprise since it was an old wood frame house. Unfortunately, one of them was burning. It wedged itself between my shoulder blades and air pack, but I couldn't get the damn thing off of me because I was too tired. My arms just couldn't do it. With the enflamed piece of wood stuck on my body, I leaned with my back in the corner of the banister of the exterior stair handles, holding the nozzle. I simply aimed it down the hallway and let it flow in the hope it would cool something down and put something out.

For the next couple of minutes, I laid there. I felt as if I was going in and out of consciousness but I can't remember for sure. One thing I do recall clearly: as I laid down holding onto the nozzle, the burning board got closer and closer to my skin until I started to feel more heat on the right side of my face.

Shit!

Then out of nowhere, Engine 44's company, Firemen O. and R. came up the stairwell and saw me. O. bent over and said, "Hey Spike!" as he pulled the wood out from between my shoulder blades and threw it on the ground.

"You alright? You look like you're having a hard time."

"I'm doing alright."

"Well shut that thing down; we're going to go in."

Following his orders, I shut the hose down. I heard the two of them inside pulling ceiling and tried to get myself together to help. In the next moment, we heard an "all-call," meaning they wanted everybody to evacuate the building because they were going to let it burn. Then we heard, "44 stays."

Aw, shit.

We looked through the floor down into the second floor and stepped on the wide parts of the charred stairwell until finally, we all made it out. I'd left the hose line in there when I left because I was running out of air and had to get another bottle. As I drank more water, I noticed that about 14 people were now resting on the tarp; earlier it had only been about eight. I sat down for a minute and saw that the house was still burning. By the time we'd reach the end of the incident, we'd use 26 pieces of apparatus.

After I changed my air pack bottle, I grabbed a hold of myself and another guy. At this point, the City of Cocoa's aerial truck had pulled up and started knocking everything down since the roof had partially burned off. We began to make headway.

B. approached me, "Hey man, we gotta go up and mop this up. Can you go in again?"

"Yeah, yeah."

Another fireman showed up and joined us. One corner on the east side was still in flames, and we knew we had to take care of it. The building had burned in a 'U' in the middle of the roof. And I was utterly exhausted as we worked to finish the job. When you're resting, you feel like you are good to go, but once you get back in to start your momentum again, you don't have it. You're totally spent.

The three of us each played a part: one fireman had the ax, I had the hose, and the other one helped us drag everything. Once we got all the way up, B. grabbed the ax, aimed it at the closed door and hit it – only to have the ax rebound and clock him in the helmet. The effort about knocked him unconscious.

"Alright, I'm done," he declared before heading back outside. The other fireman took the ax.

"Are you ready?" he asked.

"Yeah."

The plan was for him to bust the door open, then I would go in with the nozzle. After he toppled the door, he sat down, exhausted, because he'd been there fighting this thing the whole time, too. I walked in and tripped over a piece of furniture in the wholly charred room. B. crawled over toward me as I pulled myself up. We could see the sky, but fire was coming out of one corner.

"You alright?" he asked.

"Yeah."

"I'm tired."

"Me, too."

"We gotta put it out."

"I know," I conceded with a big sigh.

We crawled over to the bathroom and got on our knees. When he broke that door down, I walked into it, standing up like an idiot, and started spraying everything. When I could no longer stand, I sat down on the toilet and sprayed water all over as B. punched holes through the walls. At last, we knocked it out, and the two of us just sat there for a minute.

With the bunker gear back then, everything fell down your damn jacket – all kinds of charred wood and hot debris – absolutely everything. I ended up with a burn here and a burn there, sweating like a hog. To top it off, when they were getting the water supply, they laid in from the hydrant hose to the engine. Volunteer Engine 844 went to the marina and drew water out of the river, and the salt water made us sticky. They had drafted so much it backwashed into the city water system so people were getting saltwater out of their taps.

In my misery, I announced, "Man, I'm done." I left the hose line and walked out. Once outside, I sat on the stairs in front of the place while they started removing my equipment.

We'd arrived on-scene at 11 a.m., under summer conditions of 98-105 degrees, and finished mopping up around 5 p.m. Putting out this fire required 26 pieces of apparatus and about 32 personnel. In the end, I went through nine 30-minute air pack bottles and the only reason I used that many was because we ran out of people. It was one hell of a blaze. This incident marked the first time I ever saw them send firemen home and add others. Someone else came in and rode as a third on the Engine company with us after it was over. Although I felt terrible, I still had to finish my shift until 7 a.m. the following morning.

And we even ran more calls that day.

By the time I got back to the station, my gear was soaking wet inside and out. I removed it, took a shower, and felt clean until another call came in that required me to get back into it. It was nasty because my clothes absorbed it all. Back in the day, it used to be bravado if you had the dirtiest gear; it meant you were a workhorse. Not anymore. Now the gear carries all kinds of carcinogens, so you either throw it in a washing machine when you get back, or they come around to pick it up and give you fresh gear to wear.

In case you're wondering, the temperature inside my suit of armor could easily break 140 degrees. I remember working calls on I-95 where I could feel the heat of the road coming up and the heat from my gear coming out. It's no exaggeration to say you're literally sweating and cooking in these situations.

A WORD ABOUT AIR PACKS

The air bottle firemen wear on their backs is normal air, not oxygen. What is oxygen? Flammable. We breathe regular air. When we hook into it, they tell you the 30-minute bottle is good for 30 minutes and the 45-minute bottle is good for 45 minutes. In reality, if you're worth your salt, a 30-minute bottle is worth 20 minutes; a 45-minute bottle, 30 minutes. Once you hit 500 pounds, your buzzer goes off, and you gotta get out. You've only got 500 pounds.

If you're going into a structure and it takes 20 minutes, how long is it going to take you to get out? Twenty minutes. So you need to conserve your air. You've got a built-in system that tells you when you're at 500 pounds. You're gonna hear buzzers, you're gonna see lights telling you to head for the nearest exit. Depending on the pack and the kind of bottle (either fiberglass or steel), they usually weigh anywhere from 25 to 35 pounds.

Fire and Brimstone: The Church Fires of the Early 90s

In the early 1990s, there was an arsonist running around Merritt Island setting churches on fire. I was working with a new hire when we got paged out for a blaze at the Garden Chapel, all the way down at the end of our area. Riding jump seat behind me, L. got dressed as we flew down South Tropical. Then we heard him screaming through the slider, "I lost my mask!"

Lieutenant B. called back, "Well, grab the other one. There's one on the other jump seat."

It was nighttime. As I was driving, I could see open areas where the grass had been cut between pine trees, with a light fog on the ground. Then I smelled fire. "I think we got a burner," I remarked to my lieutenant.

"Yeah, we may have. Who knows? Who gives a fuck? Let's just get there."

When we arrived, sure enough, we found a chapel burning like hell. I rode up the driveway, went all the way around the perimeter, and stopped on the opposite end so he could see every side of it. At one time, it was a beautiful church. I got out and put on an air pack while L. grabbed the line and ran toward the fire. I finished getting dressed and followed him. Lieutenant B. pumped the truck and told everyone else what to do. Then Engine 43 arrived and laid at the corner hydrant all the way to our location to give us water. Fireman C. joined me right by the door, which had a little porch over it. We squatted down because everything above was encompassed in fire; debris rained down all around us.

When we were about ready to go in the building, we heard someone say, "Don't do it!"

It was L.

We looked back at him.

"Don't do it!"

C. and I glanced at each other and shrugged, "Screw it." We ducked down and entered the building, only to find everything engulfed in flames. L. had remained at the door feeding us hose before he finally came in too. But it wasn't long before we decided there had to be a better way; the heat was too intense for us to get very far. After a short time, the three of us backed out.

From there, we went all the way around to the end building to regroup. C. got on Engine 43 with two other guys and started pulling the hose lines for us. The rest of us grabbed a line and proceeded to the east end of the chapel, where we opened the door and walked into what appeared to be the office. Once we made it through another doorway, we were in it – the main part of the church consisting of pews and an altar. At the end, we could see the crosses on the wall. But what stopped us in our tracks for a minute was the sight of the silhouette of the flame around the main cross – which didn't appear to be actually touching it – while other flames danced on the backs of the pews. It was extraordinary. We all just sort of froze for a minute, like, *wow*.

Then we remembered, *Oh, we gotta put it out!*

We started hitting it good, which caused the conditions to worsen. Aside from thick smoke and intense heat, we had to deal with the threat of heavy timber falling on us. It had been built in the shape of a big "V" going up to the ceiling, which meant that when it burned, it got weaker and weaker, leaving us powerless to control a scenario where it eventually started crashing down. As we backed out, we heard a call for another church further up the road. Yes, somebody lit another church on fire.

Mind you, at the time, we only had a limited amount of air bottles on each Engine. On this call, we went through several. The third Engine Company that had been assisting us jumped on their truck and headed to the other church. A few minutes later, they pulled another Engine off of our fire to go to another fire over in 42's area on the other side of the island. Essentially, we had three working fires raging at the same time while we were short personnel. In the end, our church burned down. Although we put out the fire, the roof collapsed on top of it. Sadly, a wedding was supposed to take place there later that day. As for the second church, since it had just been the room and content, they got the fire under control. The third church was up in 41's area. I was familiar with it because we had run calls in there previously. Even though it had no air-conditioning, it had attracted a fantastic following; everyone wore white for services. Fortunately, the fire had only burned out the smaller room there.

At one point during our attempt to rescue Garden Chapel, we ran out of air bottles. We didn't know it at the time, but one guy on the scene still had a full one. However, he stayed down at the hydrant all night because one of his lieutenants had ordered, "Hey, you stay here." And he did. In the end, he'd been there between four- to- six hours, wearing an air pack with a full bottle. Later on, we gave him a hard time, *"Hey man, you're supposed to follow the hose back up."*

He was a good guy who didn't know any better; he just followed his lieutenant's command, with the last full bottle we had. Whether or not it would have changed the outcome, one thing I know for sure is that we definitely could have used it.

HOTTER THAN HADES: THE SUMMER FIRESTORMS OF 1998

We were at Station 43 on Merritt Island when a call came in around ten a.m. to go to Scottsmoor Mims for a brush fire. I looked at Fireman B. and remarked, "Well we ain't gonna be out there long."

"You better grab your bag," he warned.

"Really?"

"Yeah."

I did as he instructed and threw my bag in the back of the Engine. B. was driving. As we were riding along on I-95, I spotted the darkest raincloud I'd ever seen. It was *pure black* and rolling over from one side of Florida to the other.

"Wow!"

B. informed me, "That ain't rain; that's smoke."

"Holy shit!"

As he spoke, I started looking around and realized there were no cars on the Interstate. None. It was eerie, to say the least. Finally, when we got all the way up there, B. said, "You gotta find out where we're going."

I answered, "We're gonna go to Lloyds Rd."

"Are we going to the command post?"

I remembered its location, and as we rolled up, the Chief greeted us with a map. We were sitting in the Engine when he handed it to us and said, "This is where you're at. This is where you're going. This is what's coming towards you."

Three different fires burning toward each other to make one big head and become an inferno.

"That's where you're going," he repeated as he pointed to a

specific location on the map. Then he started laughing and bid us "Good luck."

Fuck.

I'd never really engaged brush fires before. Up to this point, I'd usually get there when they were simmering down, then we'd just put them out and come home. I'd never dealt with anything of this magnitude.

We rolled up to the location, saw everything coming at us, and heard the popping. Our truck was situated in a hammock, covered by oak trees; we couldn't go any further because the end of the road was soft. Then we saw two other firemen outside. The Space Center Engine went past us because their truck had four-wheel drive. As the fire got closer, we saw Canaveral go by. Now it was hell time. When we got off the truck, the fire popped up in front of us. We heard crackling, then all of the sudden, *whoosh!* A blazing inferno.

With houses on the left and right, one-thousand gallons of water, and two-and-three-quarter nozzles, we had to be careful to conserve our resources. Meanwhile, Fireman Phil and another guy were running around trying to keep the houses out of the path of destruction.

By this time, it was getting to be as hot as shit, with everything burning over and around us. *Everything* was on fire. At one point, we got back in the truck so we could breathe. Unfortunately, neither one of us had thought to put the windows up when we left, so there was no clean air to breathe. We got out, grabbed nozzles, and started hitting everything again. We would run up the driveway in between two columns of fire, trying to prevent the houses from burning. Most people don't know this, but when a fire hose is full, it grabs dirt. Since we were on a dirt road, we pulled 10-15 pounds of it, along with the hose.

B. was on one line; I was on the other. The truck was on. Conditions deteriorated so badly we just crawled underneath and sprayed water from under the truck because there was nowhere else to go. It raged all around us as we ran out of water. We didn't even bother to load the hose; we just threw it in the walk-through of the truck.

Phil's face was all black, with a trail of boogers streaming down. "That was rough!" he opined.

"Yeah!" I agreed.

All of us had watery eyes and snot-stained faces. By now, everything was burned, enabling us to see the houses we were protecting. Amazingly, we didn't lose any of them.

We loaded up the truck and drove down the road where we found a water tanker and filled it up. After spending about two hours putting out flames, we were sweaty, exhausted, and full of sand. Our bunker pants were soaked. And we still hadn't eaten anything. But when we got a call to go to a street to help two other Engine companies out, we cut out and went. As we traveled down the smaller streets, fire raged on both sides. We made a left and a right and as we proceeded, we saw houses burning up, houses starting to burn, and houses that were not yet burning. We stopped at the ones that had not yet been lit up and whenever possible, we'd attempt to extinguish the flames on those that had just caught on fire. Many times, we'd stop and look first to make a determination. You'd have to use your judgment and say, "No, it's gone," if the house had succumbed. This is the hardest decision a fireman will ever have to make because we save lives first and property second; that's what we do. But the rule is if it's burning, it's gone. Your job is to protect the ones that aren't affected, which means you have to drive past houses that are engulfed in flames. And as we drove by, we passed five- to- six houses on fire.

Approaching the end of the road, we saw an Engine company setting up and a massive wall of flame moving swiftly in our direction. We were at a "T," with one road that came through, surrounded by nothing else but woods. Then we saw another Engine – Satellite Beach – if I remember correctly, approaching. We kept watching because we were trying to figure out where we were going to set up. We looked at each other, then went back to watching them.

"They shouldn't be there," B. stated.

"No," I concurred.

Then, all of the sudden, we saw the truck turn around and speed away, leaving everybody there dragging hose. When the guys on the ground took off running toward the end of the street, I told B., "Get to U.S.1, go to U.S. 1!"

We got to U.S. 1 and made the turn. Right at that intersection in Scottsmoor Mims, there's a gas station and a row of hotel rooms.

The Battalion Chief, our Task Force leader, rolled up and announced, "We're gonna move."

I looked at B. and countered, "Bullshit, we're staying here. We're going to protect this."

We set up, fought the shit out of it, and protected those structures. Now the fire burned and went on the other side of U.S. 1, but it didn't harm the structures we guarded because everybody had positions on houses, apartments, and gas stations. We shielded Mims. The fires burned around the property but jumped the road.

That's what we did all day: go to a house, protect it, and move to the next one. We bounced around from street to street until finally we pulled up in front of a gas station because we needed fuel. By now it was around 5 p.m., and we still hadn't eaten or taken a break, but we finally got a little bit of downtime waiting for the fuel truck to roll in. Eventually, a guy came up in a mosquito control truck and filled the engine with diesel fuel. The problem was, when he'd washed his tank out with water, he didn't get all of it out. So when he pumped ours full, the engine shut off.

Then B. started vomiting. It was obvious he had to go, and we loaded him up. Next, P. started getting sick. *He* had to go. They sent out a school bus to pick up a bunch of sick, exhausted firefighters who just couldn't take it anymore. I didn't go with them because I was fine. Since the brush truck needed someone and my Engine was down, I jumped in with the driver, and we headed out to help out Engine 844. While darkness descended upon the area, the visibility of the glow tipped us off to the location of the fire.

Everything was in flames.

We arrived at Volunteer Fire Chief Joe C.'s and Engine 844's location and started fighting flames with them. Soon after, Joe went down, and they sent a Rescue to get him. Around 9 or 10 at night, I finally got on the radio to announce, "This is Spike. I need somebody to come get me, I'm done."

Tom and Devin came out in a Rescue. When I got in, they told me I looked like shit. I tried to find out about B.'s condition because he'd been pretty sick. Since he was a heavy-set guy, I thought for sure he was having a heart attack. They took me to a spot where a bus was leaving for the station and checked me out. Once I boarded, I laid against a window, where I could see the burning landscape clearly.

We finally got back to the station, where a bunch of reporters had assembled to talk to us, but all I wanted to do was push them out of the way and get some rest. Once I managed to make my way inside, there was nowhere to sleep. Nowhere to lay down. Nothing. So I went over to the bay floor against the wall, threw my coat down, and – still wearing my bunker pants – laid on the floor and fell asleep.

I woke up in the morning to B.'s big toe cracking on my nose. "Get up mother fucker!"

"Ah, you're ok!"

"Yeah, they sent me back out."

"You alright?"

"Yeah."

I got up, and as we stood there, a bunch of awesome people brought us water and food. Starving, I grabbed stuff to eat as it rolled in. B. found a cooler somewhere and threw it on our Engine, even though it was still broken down in front of the station. We could see that the cabin was tilted.

Although my shirt was crunchy, there was nothing I could do about it. I didn't have any clean clothes because I didn't know where the hell the bag was that I'd brought with me the day before.

"As soon as they get done with that Engine, we gotta get it. Everybody's waiting for it; we gotta get on it. That's *our* Engine," B. announced.

"OK."

At this point, combat-ready firemen were assembled to replace the ones who'd already been out, since that's the way it normally works in these situations. Well, the Chief saw me.

"Spike, is that your truck?" he asked.

"Yes, sir!" I responded.

"As soon as that thing gets in service, I need you to take it out to here, that fire's headed that way, it's getting ready to jump.

Get two or three other people and get the fuck out there when you can."

"Alright."

After B. spoke to the mechanics and got the Engine running, I climbed in with a few other people. Just then, Lieutenant C. approached me. "You mother fucker! You just got in there. I've been here all fucking night; I haven't been out there once. You mother fucker; who the fuck do you think you are going out in that fire again?!"

"Chief F. told me to do this."

"Oh. That's fucking bullshit! We've been waiting. We ought to do it!"

"Chief F. told me to go. I don't have time."

This lieutenant was the best guy in the world. He had every right to be pissed off, but I couldn't disobey orders by staying out of combat. With our lucky cooler on the Engine, we headed out. B. asked, "Where are we going?"

"Go here," I directed him. He floored it, and we went roaring out in that direction, where we soon saw it coming. I grabbed the hose line and ran out.

"Charge it! Charge the hose!" I yelled.

B. pulled the levers, then gave me the one-minute sign. I could see that something was wrong.

"Shit, what happened?" I asked as I watched him climb on top of the truck and then back down.

"I don't have any fucking water, they emptied it!"

He disconnected the hose, turned the engine around, and drove down a mile or two to fill the truck as the fire threatened us with all of its ferocious glory. And there we stood, C. and

I, totally defenseless, holding limp, empty hoses. I remember thinking, *What the fuck? We're like sitting ducks out here.*

By the time B. came racing back, that fire had already gone through. *Son of a bitch!* For the rest of the day, we had to chase flames. When we got out to the Dairy Queen, we saw it had been burned to the ground. In all, we stayed and fought the brush fires for two weeks.

One night, three of us went to the high school in Scottsmoor Mims to set up bunks. While there we found some basketballs, so Mighty Mike and I beat up on some Miami-Dade guys, who'd come up to help, on the basketball court. Mike, who was six-feet-tall, weighed about 140 pounds, and had a voice that sounded like Barry White crowed, "We beat them boys up."

A week or two later, I finally got off and went down to Fort Pierce where I was living at the time. And it was *still* smoky outside. My neighbors, upon seeing I had returned, brought food over. These wonderful folks gave me everything I needed. I couldn't have asked to live next door to better people.

Although the '98 brushfires were the worst I'd ever dealt with, back in the early 90s, we experienced big brush fires in Port Saint John. I remember at the time, Mike B. and I left the station and went all the way up to Lime Street to an area with all dirt roads, and houses built next to huge areas with nothing but brush everywhere.

Jim from Station 44 was one house in front of us, along with Chief T., when we pulled up.

"Drag a line to that house!" the chief ordered.

I asked, "What fucking house?" It was so smoky; you couldn't see a damn thing.

"That fucking house right there! The house is gonna catch on fire!" he bellowed.

"OK."

Mike, an older, well-respected lieutenant, grabbed the line with me. Since I was the younger one, I was the workhorse, so I dragged it down and finally found the house, where I saw two cars on fire out front. *It was as hot as hell.* All of the sudden, the flames engulfing one of the vehicles burned out of control and spread to the house. There I was, fighting to extinguish the car fire *and* the house fire while gasping for air; I couldn't breathe, due to the thickness of the smoke created by the plastics, vinyl, and rubber burning on the vehicle. Combined with the intensity of the heat, it felt surreal.

By now, Mike B. was trying to get next to me. Then, like a gift from heaven, out of nowhere came these two air packs, hitting the ground right next to us, *boom, boom!*

They arrived in the nick of time, courtesy of Fireman Jim, who knew the house was getting ready to go. Since he'd gotten his under control, he'd arrived to help us out. Gratefully, we put the air packs on while on our knees coughing and hacking, with snot streaming out of our noses and water raining from our eyes. When we finally managed to secure them on our bodies, we inhaled deeply, as if breathing clean air for the first time. In a situation like this, it usually takes a second to catch your breath before you start hitting everything you can. I remember my mask streamed up from the heat – a result of the cool air from the mask interacting with the heat from the fire. I wiped off the fog and focused on what I had to do.

We worked our way into the burning house and started putting fires out before Mike informed me he'd be back in a minute. I had no idea where he was headed, but I simply replied,

"OK." I cleaned up the house a little bit before I went back out to announce to the Chief, "We got this one down. We gotta go somewhere else."

"No. Finish here and then we'll move on," came his reply.

"OK."

Obediently, I went back in the house to find Mike. As I turned the corner, there he was, sitting on the toilet – bunker pants down and air pack on – taking a dump.

He looked at me and remarked, "It stinks in here!"

And I was like, "You mother fucker!"

When he finished taking care of business, we reloaded and went to another.

By the way, if you didn't already know, smoke inhalation is the primary cause of death for victims of indoor fires. Why? The combination of hot air and chemicals creates blisters on the back of your throat and lungs. The exposure to hot, gaseous products of combustion can cause serious respiratory complications. It's estimated that about 50-80% of fire deaths are the result of smoke inhalation injuries, including burns to the respiratory system.

CARING FOR THE GREATEST GENERATION

When I worked in Viera, a bunch of World War II veterans lived in the neighborhoods we served. One day I got a call for a structure fire and quickly arrived on the scene. Once in, I rolled my window down because I saw smoke.

"We got fire," I announced.

"Nah that's fog," one of the other fireman countered.

So I rolled my window down again and inhaled. "We got fire."

When we pulled up to the house, smoke was billowing out everywhere, including the garage, which had been filled halfway. We noticed the garage door was open, and the light was on; in fact, all of the lights were on inside the house.

"Get that line on the ground, I'll let you know in a second," I ordered.

I had been to the house before and knew that a bedridden wife lived here. I also knew we had a fire. With my air pack on, but not hooked up, I got into the house. Breathing clean underneath, I crawled under the smoke. When I got through, I saw that that the fire was in the kitchen and directed Fireman Arnie on how to proceed. Then I made a left to go into the bedroom, but the wife wasn't on the bed.

Son of a bitch.

I went around to the other side; she wasn't there either. As I crawled out, I turned left, with the burning kitchen now on my right. That's when I ran into white, winged-tip shoes and pigeon-toed feet. I reached up, made him squat down, and asked, "What are you doing?!"

"I can't find my wallet."

"Where is your wife?"

"Oh, she's at the nursing home."

Relieved, I escorted him out. It was hilarious because he walked like the comedian Tim Conway, shuffling his feet in short, brisk movements.

"Arnie! Come get this mother fucker!" I yelled. I hadn't even noticed that the guy's face was pitch black from the smoke. Rescue took a look at him and thankfully, he was fine.

Yup, sometimes being a fireman *is* about the fires.

LEARNING FROM THE BEST: SPIKE GETS A PROMOTION

"The mediocre teacher tells. The good teacher explains. The superior teacher demonstrates. The great teacher inspires."
-William Arthur Ward

For 30 years, I stayed with the Brevard County Fire Department. I like to think many people liked me as a fireman, and many people liked me as a lieutenant. I worked as a fireman for fifteen years, putting off my promotion to lieutenant for as long as possible, on purpose. Because as a fireman, you can't really hurt anybody, but as a lieutenant, you have the ability to hurt multiple people with one bad decision. That's why I wanted to spend as much time as I could, learning from the best.

And I did.

From one lieutenant, I learned about honor and respect. From another, I learned fragility. I picked up valuable lessons just by watching how other people ran the show. I can't say there was any one person who taught me how to be a lieutenant, but there was one person who taught me how to be a leader: Joe M. He and I were great friends for a bit until we butted heads and I decided to go to another station. When I left, he actually helped me more because I had already learned a tremendous amount from him.

Joe held you up to a standard. If you weren't meeting that standard, he tried to bring you up to it. If you couldn't attain it, he'd tell you that you should probably be doing something else. He never said anything like that to me since my work was consistently good – unlike outside of the department, where I was always failing at something else in my personal life, especially relationships.

Another lieutenant stands out for forcing me to strive for the next level because his leadership was not up to par; it was as if they had been giving badges out one day and he got one. He wasn't a bad person, just not equipped for the job. Whenever we had a rookie, the rookie looked to me, not to him. *I* made the decisions. Many people depended on me to take care of what needed to be done. That's when I decided to go for the promotion, figuring, "If he can do it, I can do it."

One day, I took the test after studying diligently in preparation. And when the results came back via email, I was number one. Shocked, I emailed back, "OK, send the real ones."

The answer? "Trust me, I checked it three times. You are number one."

At the time, I was in medic school. Now, I'm a three-time failure at medic school because I don't like being a medic. I never will. Medic is just not for me. But I tried it because it's not whether you hit the ball out of the park; it's a matter of whether or not you try to hit it. And I took the medic test three times. When the Chief came down to visit us at the school, the other guys kept asking him, "Is he gonna get promoted? Is he gonna get promoted?"

The Chief answered, "Let Spike ask me that."

And I was like, "Nope." I wouldn't ask. It was up to him.

He could've skipped over me and picked a medic to promote, but he didn't. He promoted me.

Since there was an opening, I got placed at Station 63 in Indialantic, where I had the best crew anyone could ask for. They broke me into my new role and every morning, we bonded over a breakfast of biscuits and gravy, and bacon and eggs. After six months, a position opened in Viera at Station 47, a Special Ops House. It had hazmat – something I wanted nothing to do with. However, I had to move out of Station 63, and Viera was the only permanent opportunity available in the county.

As soon as I walked in, I met with Lieutenant G., a phenomenal hazmat specialist, and told him, "Look, man, I don't want nothing to do with that hazmat. I'll stay on that Engine forever." At the time, his wife was pregnant with their second child, so this arrangement worked out well for him.

He replied, "OK, but you are gonna have to get on it once in a while."

I remained on that Engine, which ran a significant amount of calls – about 15-19 per shift – until I retired. Needless to say, we generally didn't sleep much, which was why I got into the habit of going to bed early; I'd get a little bit of rest and downtime in the lull right after dinner. Of course, the guys would mess with me about it.

A CHRISTMAS MIRACLE

It was Christmastime, 2013. At this point, I was an officer *and* a lieutenant, working on a call for someone who was having chest pains. While on the scene, I heard the radio crackle back and forth about another call going on in my area. They asked if I was available but I couldn't leave because I didn't have a Rescue there yet. I listened as they directed Rescue 80 and Engine 80 – who were on U.S. Route 1 on the other side of the river – to the site. I knew they had quite a distance to travel, so when our Rescue pulled in, we gave them the rundown on the patient.

"Can you handle it?" I asked. "We got another call coming in."

"Yeah."

We got in the Engine, and I radioed, "Go ahead with the traffic. What do you have for me?"

It was a pedestrian who'd been struck by a vehicle. Believe it or not, in most cases, someone getting hit by a car is minor; you sort of play it off a little bit. Well, it was my mistake. I asked dispatch, "Who do you have responding so far?"

"Engine 80 and Rescue 80."

"Go ahead and cancel them."

Our excellent dispatch challenged me, "Um, you sure you want to cancel? Maybe you should keep them coming."

"OK, keep 'em coming. Maybe they'll beat us there."

My crew and I rushed over in the Engine, heading north on A1A. As we approached the scene, there was a gentleman laying out in the road. His body was contorted and misshapen with a broken humerus, forearm, and legs…completely bent out of shape. Still sitting inside the truck, I made a call, "Brevard Engine 62 on scene; gonna issue a trauma alert. Get me a chopper and we'll go ahead and land him behind my station." I made that decision because my station was only two minutes away.

My guys packaged the victim, got him to the back of the Rescue, and transported him to the LZ (landing zone) in *less than* nine minutes.

When a trauma alert is issued, there's a thing called *The Golden Hour* – the faster they can arrive and get the patient to an emergency room within the hour, the better the chances of survival. Unlike trauma involving broken bones only, most of the time, severe trauma cases don't end up coming around and walking. Often with severe trauma, the cases are fatal, although with today's EMS system and equipment there tend to be more favorable outcomes.

In this case, we found out the guy was 18 years old. He'd been jogging on the sidewalk along A1A in the evening and got hit as soon as he stepped out into traffic to cross the road. It's one of the darkest portions of A1A in Satellite Beach. He was so messed up we didn't think he was gonna survive. In a credit to the crew – Mike and the guys – he pulled through. They legitimately saved his life.

Six months later, we heard he had stopped by the station. In all of my years of service, it's extremely rare for anyone to come by to say thank you. It's not because they have to, and it's not what we're looking for. But for all intents and purposes, this kid was dead, and my guys saved him.

Right before my retirement in November of 2014, almost a full year to the day he was struck, he walked into my station laughing; it was good to see him. He looked amazing. The accident left him with some deficits, for example, he is blind in his right eye. And when he's riding with his sister in the car, he'll point and say, "Turn here," obviously joking because he can't see. He also has some deficit in his left arm, which was severely damaged, but he told us he was working hard in physical therapy to get it back.

His recovery is a testament to Engine Rescue 80 – Johann and his crew. My crew. All working together to get him where he needed to be. That's a sign of constant training, of knowing how to do your job, of teamwork, of everything that the departments are made up to do. Working in unison, the way they're supposed to, to get the desired outcome. It was perfect; one of the best stories of my career.

HOLIDAY TERROR ON TROPICAL TRAIL

We were at the station when we got a call to respond to an incident involving a vehicle hitting a pedestrian on Tropical Trail. Arriving on-scene, we discovered it was a little kid, probably about 10 years old. He had run out in front of traffic and was struck by a vehicle at about 40 – 45 m.p.h. Unfortunately, his family was there and witnessed the entire accident – including his father, who was a doctor. We rolled up and got to the patient while his dad yelled, "He has a bleed, he has a bleed!"

As soon as I got out of the truck, I heard the commotion and ordered my medics to examine him immediately. Then I called a trauma alert, which was issued right away. Depending on time, location, and traffic route, you ask for a helicopter. On the way there, I'd already told them to put a helicopter on standby. With a trauma alert, you need somebody to land the aircraft, which is why you have to get another Engine and a deputy to come in and block the roads; you take ownership of a piece of land so that the chopper can touch down. In this case, it landed just south of Pineda Causeway, along South Tropical Trail, right there. My guys did everything they could to save the boy, whose pupils were fixed and blown, with a little bit of blood trickling from his mouth.

This was a week before Christmas.

As the family looked on, I heard the dad screaming and the mom breaking down while torturous thoughts echoed through my mind. The medics worked diligently in close proximity to get a line on him. When Jessie pulled a brand-new needle out of the catheter at the same time Chad moved his gloved hand backwards, it struck the clean needle. Undaunted, he pulled his hand away with the catheter sticking out, stopping for a second to look at her and remark, "Really?" before resuming his task.

Despite their best efforts, the kid didn't make it.

We get called after the worst events happen. *The worst time in your life.* At no time have I ever heard of a firefighter, an EMT, or a medic arriving on scene with the intention of doing more damage to somebody who has already been critically injured.

A week later, we ran another trauma alert in that same area, right around New Years. In the early morning of a nice day, we were in quarters doing a truck check-out and goofing off when we got a call for a bicyclist down on South Tropical Trail, south of Pineda Causeway.

As we headed to the accident in the vehicle, I got good info. A bystander there told me what was going on: agonal respirations, unresponsive. Before I even arrived, I had a clear sense of what we'd find. Per our rules and regulations, we're not allowed to ask for a chopper unless we're on the scene. But knowing the flight time and the idea that I needed another Engine, I requested, "Send me Engine 80 and a chopper. We're gonna land him on South Tropical."

As we came off of Pineda and onto South Tropical, we made a couple turns and saw the victim laying on the ground with two other cyclists nearby. Just as the witness had described, we found him unresponsive with agonal respirations and multiple contusions and abrasions to his face, elbows, and hands. His clavicle was broken, and he had a pneumothorax (air in the lung cavity, which forces the lung to collapse); gray matter oozed out of his ear.

Once again, my guys, because they are the best, got him

packaged. I talked to bystanders while this was going on. Before he'd even arrived on Engine 80, Lieutenant Johann had asked over the radio, "Hey, we going to the same spot as the kid?"

"That's affirmative."

He remembered because these two incidents had occurred within a week of each other. And just as with the young boy, this guy didn't make it either. We later found out he was a prominent man in the area and only 51 years old.

MUTUAL AID, KINGS, AND KINGDOMS

I've been on fire calls where another call comes in, and you have to throw everything on the truck and leave to put out a different fire. I've been on many fire calls where a unit that's on its way to assist us gets diverted to extinguish another one that has broken out. Thankfully, auto-aid and mutual aid have gotten much better. For example, if the City of Rockledge needs help, we'll automatically respond to their area and vice-versa. Mutual aid means Rockledge will radio and say, "Hey, we need help. Can you help us?" and we send an Engine. Auto-aid means if our station is across from a city station and they need help, we'll go help. Each city has to sign an agreement saying, "I'll cover you, you cover me." However, since certain cities don't like playing with others here in Brevard, they refuse to sign it in an act of pure politics. Each department has their own kingdom, and in that kingdom, the king is king. And if the king doesn't want another king sharing his throne, even when it's a matter of life and death, he won't sign the agreement. Ah, the games we play.

The guys on the street? We don't care. We're gonna go anyway; we're gonna be there. When I was at 47, if I heard something breaking loose in Rockledge, I'd go. One time, when they had a big brush fire, I was working at Station 47 in Viera; Rockledge was within my reach. I heard the chatter on the radio that all three of their stations were out attending to brush fires and conditions were worsening. I told my guys, "Go get on the Engine."

"Why? It's in Rockledge."

"Go, get on the Engine. We're gonna end up there anyway; let's start going."

As we were driving, the radio broke in, "Engine 47 Brevard."

I responded, "Brevard Engine 47, we're en route."

What happens is, if all of their stations are busy, we'll roll into the city and pick up their calls. So if somebody gets sick or another fire's going, we can cover it. At the time, my dispatch was good. I always worked well with them anyway: I knew what they were doing, and they knew what I was doing.

"Engine 47 Brevard, respond City of Rockledge."

And they gave me the address. Before that, I'd been driving normally, but now I could upgrade by throwing the lights on.

"Responding."

We raced north up Murrell, a four-lane highway, toward Rockledge. As we got closer, we saw the column of smoke and noticed less and less traffic on the road. The problem at the time was that the City of Rockledge and county units couldn't talk on the same radio. They were in the middle of transitioning the radio system to where everyone would have the 800 system.

"Get to District 17 and get a radio from them so you can communicate," came the order.

In the middle of Murrell Road, surrounded by dense smoke, I got out of the Engine and tried to locate them. I had to walk because I couldn't see as I yelled, "District 17, where are you?!"

Thankfully, he found me. "Here's the radio," he announced as he handed it to me and told me where to go. Now I had his radio in one pocket and mine in another. I turned around, found my way back through the smoke, and got on the Engine.

"We gotta go here," I informed my driver.

As we rolled up, one of my Chiefs greeted me. "Can you get with that district and see if they need a task force?"

Meanwhile, we had flames approaching structures and hose lines deployed. Two of my guys were on two different hose lines while the fire raged right at us. And here was this Chief, asking me to get a hold of them. I was like, "Negative. I can't do it, I'm busy."

Then the District Chief of Rockledge radioed, "How are you guys doing over there?"

"We got a lot of fire coming this way. It's gonna hit the fan here in a minute. I'll get back with you just give me some time," I responded.

"Do you need anything?"

"No. I'd start asking for more."

"I already am."

"Copy."

"Let me know what you need."

"Alright, give me a minute. It's not *getting* here; it *is* here."

The idea with a brush fire is if your house is backed up to an empty lot, we want it to burn all the way up to the end of that lot. Why? It needs to fuel up so it's no longer a hazard for us. We use the water to protect the house from burning, but we're not gonna put the woods out. If the house catches fire, we're gonna use the water on the house. Or, if it's starting to get too hot, we'll cool the house down with it.

On this day, the fire burned all the way up to the end of the lot while we wet the house a little bit, using our water supply sparingly. In the end, we used 750 gallons.

Then my driver returned to announce, "I located a hydrant, I'm going to drop 200 feet to it."

The conditions were so bad you couldn't see where the hydrants were. In fact, you could barely see anything. Back then, we had map books, not computers, and since I didn't have one for the City of Rockledge, I had no way of determining the location of a hydrant. Fortunately, my engineer had been smart enough to just do a good walk-around while we were waiting and deploying hose lines. Ultimately, he found one and made a hook-up. Now we could just start hitting everything using all the water we wanted.

I called back the District for Rockledge. "We're good over here. I got a water supply, we got hoses and we're running. We're doing fine."

"Copy that. Thank God."

Remember, I was holding two radios. After I spoke to the Rockledge District, my Chief called to see what I needed. I alternated from one radio to another saying, "No, we're good," to one in my right hand and one in my left.

Later, my Chief and another Chief pulled in. "You guys need water?"

"No, we're good."

In all, we stayed there about two- to- three hours helping Rockledge out. I'm happy to report we didn't lose any structures; everything was fine. In my experience as a lieutenant, I learned the importance of listening to the radio and knowing when and how you're going to be needed. Being ahead of the game is crucial;

you cannot wait for the call. You have to be proactive and realize you're gonna have to go.

I employed the same strategy with an auto accident on I-95. If I heard 80 running a shitty call on the Interstate, if I was near their area I was already on my way. I backed up 44 and 80, and 44 and 80 backed up me. If they heard something going down with my Engine, they would be on their way to assist. We worked unbelievably well together in that area – 80, 81, 44 – we were a solid, effective team.

Of course, everybody's proud of their own station: 44 was the Irish guys; 81 was a bunch of hunters, and Viera? We were the rich kids because we had hazmat.

We always got razzed, "Hazmat crews, you're so special. Oh, you guys are special ops."

Then there were the practical jokes.

Once, we were out on a structure fire all night so 44 got pulled to come to our station. When we returned from the call, we cleaned up and went to bed. Nobody noticed it, but when we got up, our coffee maker was gone: 44 had taken it.

There we were, 16 battle-weary guys, and when we got up in the morning, we had no coffee maker. A new shift was coming on, we were getting ready to go off, and all we had was a Mr. Coffee, just pumping away, trying to make as much as it could. The funny thing was, the plug on it didn't work, which meant somebody had to cut the plug to bare the wires to plug them into the outlet. We all sat there patiently, waiting for this little thing to brew coffee at a painstaking rate of one cup at a time. It was pull the pot out, put your cup under.

Although pissed off, we tried to be better and agreed not to retaliate. But 44 hadn't just messed with our coffee. Another time, they set the remote on the TV to change the channel every 20 minutes. So you'd be watching a show and just before it ended, the remote would automatically switch to a different channel.

They would also move stuff around our station or take it altogether, then send us pictures of it. You'd have to go hunt it down – *on your day off, not with taxpayer money.*

Our chance to pay them back arrived one day when we got sent up to 44's area. I was at Station 44; Station 43 had just cleared a fire they'd been on with 44, but 44 had to stay on the scene.

When 43 came back, I looked at Fireman F. and asked, "Has 44 ever messed with your shit?"

"All the time."

"Wanna get 'em back?"

"Yeah, what do you wanna do?"

"Let's take every bit of furniture they have and set it up in the bay where they gotta pull the trucks in."

"That's fuckin' awesome!"

We started moving furniture the way we found it. If there were keys sitting on a table, that's exactly how it went out. It was perfect. We set everything in the bay just as it had been arranged inside.

Then District 40 came by, looked in, and started laughing, "What the fuck are you guys doing?"

"Well, they always fuck with us so we're fuckin' with them."

"That's hilarious! Everything's in the bay just like it was in the station."

We even placed the TV in the corner. It was perfect. Engine 43 and us were both pulled out front of the station with the back bay doors closed. They had released us to go back to quarters.

"Copy."

So we sat in our Engines and waited, having left the front door open. As the back door lifted, we saw the guys look at the bay and exclaim, "Oh fuck! You mother fuckers!"

We just laughed. Every bit of their furniture – the bunks, kitchen table, everything – was out in the bay.

Chief L. cracked up too. Their lieutenant asked, "Goddammit! Aren't you gonna do something?"

"No," the Chief replied. "You fuck with them all the time. About time you got payback."

When all is said and done, every Engine has pride: pride in your equipment and pride in your station. We'd compete over who had the cleanest trucks, bays, and stations; who had run the most calls; and who beat who to the call first. Later on, toward the end of my career, they let us wear pride shirts like "The Beast of the East," or "The Beach House." Ours at Station 47 was "The Zoo," in reference to our location right by the Brevard Zoo. Each station had their own gig. At times, we experienced true brotherhood among all of the stations and other times, not so much. But I loved that they allowed each one to wear pride shirts, which motivated us to work even harder.

NEVER FORGET: SEPTEMBER 11, 2001

> "The tragedy of life and of the world is not that men do not know God; the tragedy is, that knowing Him, they still insist on going their own way."
> -William Barclay

I was on duty when the Towers got hit. We were dealing with a call at a La Quinta Hotel, where some guy tried to overdose because his girlfriend broke up with him…whatever. All he was doing was crying out for attention. When we went over to take care of the crybaby, we had to wait in the hallway because the cops were talking to him. The next thing I knew, a maid came out of one of the rooms to tell us, "Somebody just crashed a plane into the World Trade Center."

My buddy Brock answered in his thick New York accent, "Whoa, that's gotta be a bad pilot cuz them things are huge! I doubt that happened."

Well, we got this yahoo out of the hotel room and were in the process of putting him on the stretcher when he took off. We caught him, tackled him, and laid him back down. While we secured him to the stretcher, the maid came back out to announce, "A plane just hit the second tower."

Brock and I looked at each other in disbelief. A New York native who was relatively new to Florida, he had tons of friends and family up there. In fact, he still traveled to the area quite a bit. We finished the call and got the guy to the back of the rig, which transported him to the hospital. Then we returned to the station, where the news was on. As soon as we walked in, we realized it was true: the towers were burning. Brock was out of his mind. He sat there rubbing his head for a while, then grabbed his cell phone to call a couple of guys he knew, but couldn't make a connection. In the next moment, the towers collapsed.

While events unfolded that day, we ran calls, trying to get back to the station as quickly as possible after each one. We wanted to stay updated about all the shit that was going down. At one point, Brock and I laid on our side-by-side bunks in a dark room, with the light from the TV hitting us as we watched the news reports.

He turned to me and announced, "I'm fucking leaving tomorrow morning. I gotta go. I gotta go. I'm going, I'm going."

Then we got a page and an email from our Chief: "If you need to go, or you feel like you need to go up there, you got family or something, and you wanna go, call me and put in for the time and we'll get you out."

Brock and I put in for the time and left the next morning.

The only reason I went was because Brock was out of his mind. His son, who had just turned eighteen and was not yet a fireman, came with us. Riding up on I-95, Brock never even looked straight ahead; he constantly talked and looked over at me. He drove by feel – bump, bump, bump! – to determine whether he had to go left or right on the road while driving at 100 m.p.h. the entire time. Good thing there wasn't that much traffic. Once en route, we didn't stop until we got to a hotel just outside of New York, where we stayed for about two hours to get some sleep. Unfortunately, Brock snored like a buzz saw, making it impossible for me to get any rest.

The next morning, we drove to the Lincoln Tunnel and ended up being the third car in line. In front of us was a pickup truck with strobes in the back that blinded me the whole time. The vehicle ahead of them was a Port Authority car. When I got out to talk to the EMS guys up front, I walked by the truck and said: "Hey man, kill your strobes." While I was standing at the driver's side door, the Port Authority cop got out, took one look at me and asked, "You FD?"

"Yeah, we're from Florida. I got two more in the truck."

"When that thing opens, you guys get right behind me."

The EMS workers inside the truck spoke up to alert him to their presence as well. "Ok, both of you guys, follow me in as soon as it opens up," he instructed.

The Lincoln Tunnel opened for 20 minutes. It seemed as if they immediately closed it after we cleared because of another bomb threat. As we pulled onto Broadway, we noticed just a few cars. Manhattan looked like a ghost town, reminiscent of one of those movies where everybody flees the city. We drove by Jacob Javits Convention Center on Chelsea Pier, where hundreds of Rescues were lined up. The EMS workers peeled off there while we headed to the command post. I can't remember exactly where it was, but as I recall it was nearby.

When we reported to the command post *like we were supposed to* the lady asked, "Are you paid or volunteer?"

"Paid."

"Where are you from?"

"Florida."

Brock and I each carried fanny packs containing all of our certifications, as we were required to do when on duty. OSHA (Occupational Safety and Health Administration) mandates a copy of our certs and numbers; if you ran a call, they would always come down to investigate, and you had to show them that paperwork. So we presented it to her and watched as she went through it: "You're confined space, hazmat, ropes. You guys are special ops."

"Well, yeah," I confirmed.

"Go get in whatever you drove and get out in the street. You're gonna have a squad car and they're gonna take you in."

My jaw hit the ground. I did not expect to be doing that.

When you do big shit like a cruise ship fire, all you really do is stage. You're sitting there, shuttling bottled water, moving it around, you know, because if they need it, you get it. That's what I thought we would be doing, but no, we got assigned to help with search and recovery.

We found a squad car and got assigned to a battalion…well, first we answered phones at a school, *then* we got assigned to a battalion. Literally, the battalion boss came in and declared, "We need you to go in; you gotta find somebody to do what you're doing."

Mind you, there was no power. It had gone out in the aftermath of the attack, so they brought a portable AC unit into the facility to cool everyone off. It was the morning of September 13, and this battalion chief looked exhausted. His white shirt was gray from all the debris. He told us he had a twin brother who was another battalion chief somewhere else in the city.

Then, in the next moment, out of nowhere a doctor and two nurses walked up and announced, "Hey, we're here to help. What can we do?"

It was as if God had just answered our prayers, "*I sent them to you. Let them do what you're doing.*"

And we did. We showed them, and they took over.

Our battalion lined up, and we embarked upon a 30-40-minute walk to get to where we needed to be. Along the way, we went through some damage-riddled buildings. One had a big atrium with palm trees all over the place; it looked like Florida, but you could see where it had collapsed. Then there was a mini-mall/walkway about 16 feet wide, with sunlight streaming in toward its end. As we moved in that direction, we trudged through some water and what looked like oatmeal but was a mixture of dust and water. A two-and-a-half-inch hose line ran all the way out. When I noticed that all the way up front, people were stepping over to the side and removing their helmets, I pushed Brock's kid over to the wall and told him to take his helmet off. In the next moment, they brought a fallen fireman by who'd been killed in the collapse. It whipped us back to reality for a second.

As we continued, there was the last skyway. The walkway was still up, and all kinds of people were just sitting around because they'd been working there the entire time. When we turned the corner and made it underneath, that's when it opened up: as far as you could see, the damage was horrific. I just sat there like, *Holy cow!* I didn't know what to say. Then the biggest guy I'd ever seen came up, leaned me forward, read my shirt, and remarked in a heavy New York accent, "*Brevahd County?* Where the fuck is that?"

Now I am 6' 2" tall, and I was looking almost straight up at this guy. He was huge.

"In Florida," I answered.

He stuck his hand out to shake mine, then put his other arm around me. "I'm glad you're here. Let's go get some of our brothers."

My lip quivered and my eyes watered. *Wow.*

Approaching the place where they wanted us to set up and start digging, we saw a completely vacated ambulance with all of the doors open. Obviously, the people who'd been in it just took off when everything went to hell. Inside, it was full of dust and debris, with compartments thrown open from all the wind and a cracked windshield. There was a twisted firetruck nearby, along with air packs laying on the ground. Combined with the debris from the building, everything just got to me; I was totally overwhelmed. My senses, *everything*, completely shut down until I had no feeling about what I was doing. It was as if I was on auto-pilot; I wasn't even thinking. I'd see what somebody else was doing and robotically mimicked their actions.

Because we were special ops with the battalion, we ended up digging at different spots, finding voids, and going down into holes, trying to locate stuff. In some cases, you smelled something. In others, you didn't. Although the safest way to walk was on the beams, they weren't always solid. I took a fall, and when I did, I put my hand down to brace myself, broke my pinky, and sliced my hand. But I kept digging.

After about 17 hours, we walked out. Another guy saw us and asked, "*Brevahd County*, where the hell is that?"

Brock turned around and exclaimed, "Joey!"

"Brocko!"

They actually knew each other. As I'd discover during our time at Ground Zero, Brock really did know a lot of guys in New York. He proved me wrong; he wasn't a typical macho man running off his mouth.

"Hey, how'd you guys get in here?" Joey asked.

We told him we got assigned a battalion. But when they'd

called it after about 12 or 13 hours, we stayed longer to keep digging.

"How did you get in?"

"We got in a pickup truck."

"Can me and Cap ride back with you guys? Cuz, nobody's leaving."

"Sure."

By now the sun was setting. It wasn't yet dark, but there was a beautiful orange light illuminating Manhattan – a spectacular scene. As we made our way out, we saw one of those little dust devils, a whirlwind that forms when hot air near the surface rises quickly through a small pocket of cooler, low-pressure air above it. While rare in places like New York, keep in mind the temperature that day was somewhere around 100 degrees. It was *hot*, the hottest I've ever been in this city.

But let me tell you how I feel about New York: these people are the best in the world. At the worst time in their history, when they'd been pushed to the limit, they stepped over that limit and went straight up to the sky with whatever they could do. On one side of the road there were generators; then in another section on the same side, chainsaws. *Brand-new*, with the tags hanging off. On the other side of the road, every one of the five-star restaurants had set up buffets where they were heating and cooking food with Sterno. As soon as they saw us, they handed us plates, food, and drinks. I still had my helmet on as I carried my coat and sported a broken finger. And they stuffed my pocket with a loaf of bread, a bottle of Gatorade, and food.

Since I could only carry so much, we sat down on the sidewalk to eat, absolutely filthy. We were covered from head to toe with white dust; sweat stuck on us like a paste, filling in the cracks of our necks. We smelled like ash, and our shirts were so stiff, they were crunchy. Starving, we ate like we'd never eaten before.

Finally, it was time to get in the truck. Because Cap was an older guy, he rode shotgun with Brock's son in the middle. Brock drove, and Joey and I sat tailgate. Going through the city, we still had our bunker pants and shirts on. There was barely any traffic, but people came up behind us, beeping horns and giving us the thumbs-up. If stopped on a corner long enough, they would come running out with bottles of water.

I remember waiting at an intersection where people just started touching us. I guess they wanted some kind of reality out of our presence; solid confirmation we were truly there to help them. I'll never forget one lady, in particular, a beautiful brunette who was dressed in a mid-thigh business skirt and white shirt, with black stockings and glasses. She'd been crossing the street and paused to look at us before she just fell to her knees and cried out in pure anguish.

Wow.

I looked at Joey with tear-stained eyes and saw that he was also choked up. As we wiped our faces, we yelled at each other, "You need to fucking stop!"

When we finally got all the way down to Truck 25 House (in Florida, we call them Stations, in New York they call them Houses), Brock and I stayed outside discussing what we were going to do because we were so dirty. All of the sudden, some guy came running out of the House screaming, "You fuckas, you mother fuckas! Get the fuck!"

I looked at Brock, "What did you do?"

"I didn't do nothing."

The guy urged, "Get the fuck in here; we got food!"

I walked in like Pig Pen from the Peanuts comic strip with my bunker pants on, surrounded by a cloud of dust. Since Truck 43 was in the middle of the road, cars were driving on the sidewalk and around the vehicles to get to the street. It was the craziest thing I ever saw.

Once inside, I ate again. One of the guys at the House informed us, "Hey listen, we can't put you guys up. We got 30 guys here already. We just don't have room. But, there're two hotels giving out rooms. One of them is right there," as he spoke he pointed to the On the Avenue Hotel, "and there's another one further down the road."

Well, since I was exhausted, I decided to go for the closer option. When I entered the lobby of the On the Avenue Hotel, there was a line at the front desk. After patiently waiting for my turn, I said to the clerk, "I heard you guys were giving out rooms."

She replied, "Ok, who are you with?"

"The Fire Department."

In a low voice, she continued, "I know. Go over there and use that phone. Dial this number."

"OK."

I did as instructed; as the phone rang in my ear, I heard it ringing behind the front desk. She picked up and greeted me, "On the Avenue Hotel."

"It's me over here in the bunker gear. You guys said you were giving rooms out."

"Ok. Here's your confirmation number. Bye."

When I walked back over, she apologized, "Sorry about that. It's the only way we can do it."

I got a separate room from Brock because of my desperate

need for uninterrupted sleep.

The next day in uniform back at House 25, a choir came by and set up a memorial with flowers to honor six of their guys who'd been lost. The dusty, dirty truck they'd ridden in had come back. People came by and lit candles while the choir sang beautiful songs.

We stayed a little longer, went back to the site, and dug some more.

On the way home to Florida, we stopped to see Brock's brother, who worked for the FBI and had been over at the Pentagon. When met him in his hotel lobby, it was obvious he'd been up all night. Visibly shaking, he told us stories of how he was opening doors to find dead people still sitting at their desks. We all cried together.

The trauma had been positively unnerving. Luckily, with the exception of Brock's son, we'd all been around gruesome, horrific scenes like this before. Of course, nothing on such a grand scale, but at least we had some sort of preparation. On the way home, we really didn't say much until we pulled in around one a.m.

I jumped in my car to drive home, not even bothering to put the radio on. When I walked into my house, the first thing I did was crawl into bed, and as soon as I woke up the next morning, I called my parents to say, "I'm home."

My dad replied, "I want you to come down here to Fort Pierce and relax."

At the time, my little brother was an on-air radio personality. Throughout my time in New York, he called often to ask about what was going on. To this day, I don't know if he ever divulged anything I told him on the radio; I'd just assumed he wanted to check on me.

Soon after arriving at my parents' home, I got a call from one of the chiefs.

"What are you doing? Where are you at?"

"I'm in Fort Pierce with my parents."

"Well, you need to be up here."

"Why do I need to be up there?"

"Because the news wants to talk to you."

"Did you call Brock?"

"No, I don't like talking to Brock."

"Well you call Brock, and if he wants to do it, then I'll do it. If not, we're out."

"You guys have to do it! So you need to call Brock, and you need to be up here by one o'clock."

At that point, it was already Noon.

"That's not gonna happen," I told him. "If you want us to be there it'll have to be three-thirty."

Reluctantly, I got in the car and drove all the way back to Brevard. Since they wanted us in uniform, we had to put them on. At the press conference, we were greeted with about 50 microphones and multiple reporters firing questions at us.

I remember one clearly, "When do you think they're going to get them off the pile?"

"They're not getting those guys off the pile. That's not what happens. There'll be a fight to get those firemen off of there. They are not coming off there until they find the last one. Then they'll get off. But not until then," I answered.

And sure enough, up in Manhattan, a huge fight broke out later on down the road between cops and firemen when the cops tried to keep them from the pile. They went to fisticuffs because the firemen would not stay away, and a bunch of them even got arrested. It was crazy.

A day or two later, I went back to work at the station. Somewhere in the middle of everything, we went to a funeral for one of our medics, Roland, who'd passed away. While at the services, Florida Today asked us to do interviews with them, which is how our pictures ended up in the paper. I had no idea the problems this would cause for me.

A few days after that issue of Florida Today came out, Brock and I started to receive awful phone calls. Hate email. Death threats. Bomb threats. Battalion chiefs derided the two of us as *Free* and *Lance*, as in *freelance*. Most of the vitriol came from within Brevard, some of it from out of town.

Everybody wanted to go to Ground Zero. Everyone wanted to be there. And I don't blame them.

But I look at it this way: if you're going to call somebody your brother, and he truly is your brother, are you gonna hide behind excuses like, *I gotta cut grass, my wife won't let me,* or *I gotta get the kids to school?*

Are you going to fault *me* because I *didn't* wait to go up there to help my brother out? And if it is your brother, then you should've been standing next to me on that pile – not standing at home pointing fingers at me.

Fuck you for not calling me and asking about what happened.

As a lieutenant, I had a responsibility to the people I worked with; to make sure they got home safely at the end of shift. If I saw that one of my guys was drinking too much, I was going to intervene, whether he was on- or off-duty. If I saw that one of my guys needed help, on- or off-duty, I was going to give him a hand. The only reason I went up there to help was to keep Brock out of trouble. Where we ended up and how we ended up where we did is no secret. We signed in at the command post. We did everything the way we were trained to do it.

The only thing we didn't wait for was for somebody to call and say, "Hey, your brother's in trouble but we're gonna wait two weeks before we pull you up there."

If you're gonna call this brotherhood shit, then when a man falls, and it's your brother, be there to pick him up. Don't sit here and bitch at somebody else who *is* picking him up. That's what pissed me off so badly. I got a retired FDNY guy calling me, bitching me out, asking me if I really think I made a difference.

Now I can tell you, I did.

We sacrificed our time, spent our own money, and risked our own lives going up there to help people we didn't even know. That *I* didn't know.

You're posing standing over the bodies of dead brothers. That's what they said to us.

It wasn't even a pose. And if they were your brothers, then you should have been standing with me.

All these years later, I think I deserve my say.

Some of the guys complaining about me belonged to a fraternal order. A few of them knew me personally, yet not one came to my defense or even bothered to call to ask what happened. At the Christmas party that year, I got into a big brawl. After that I was done; I wasn't going to take it anymore. *If you wanna fight me, just line up. Line up. Get it over with.* That was my attitude. There's still a guy down at Palm Bay Fire Department who likes to take his cheap shots. To this day. Every year when it comes around, he'll put something in the paper anonymously. But he doesn't have the guts to step forward and identify himself. Coward.

On the positive side, my experience at Ground Zero taught me to never take my loved ones for granted. From then on, I made it a point to tell my parents, my little brother, my daughter, my friends, and the special woman in my life I loved them. When I was married, I'd say "I love you" with a hug and a kiss before going to sleep, and in the morning, before we went our separate ways, I'd hug and kiss her, and tell her I loved her. Because life is fragile and unpredictable. In my line of work, I know that better than anybody.

PTSD: THE ETERNAL STRUGGLE

"Courage does not always roar. Sometimes courage is the quiet voice at the end of the day saying, 'I will try again tomorrow.'"
– Mary Anne Radmacher

To think that doctors, nurses, firemen, police officers, and paramedics don't have PTSD is just a little ridiculous. The difference between us and the military – not that they're even comparable – is that the military goes away to fight their battles. They've lost their buddies, they've experienced horrific events, they've risked their lives, they've been shot at regularly, and then they get to come home. When they return, they need PTSD assistance, and they should get it everywhere.

For firefighters, cops, nurses and everybody else, our battlefield is here. The military fights the battles overseas; emergency service workers and police battle them right here at home. If a fireman, medic, cop, nurse or doctor claim that they have not been bothered by the horrific cases they've worked on, they are lying. And if they're telling the truth, they should be in another line of work. Because as human beings, everything we do is based on feelings; you legitimately feel what these people are going through – the pain, anguish, and loss.

On top of that, when you lose co-workers you shouldn't be losing to natural causes, it hits home and dredges up the reservoir of unresolved emotion. Even something as simple as a smell or a sound, or the commonplace activity of driving down a roadway where I've dealt with a fatality will transport me right back to the intensity of the moment, no matter how long ago it occurred. Sometimes, it will freeze me right where I'm at.

As fire and police, the problem we have with the realm in which we work in is that there is no escape. You can never erase from your mind the grotesque scenes you have witnessed, much like our brothers and sisters in the military. Yet first responders are left to cope with PTSD on their own, even after retirement. Eventually, it builds up to a breaking point.

As I stated at the beginning, when you're working and on insurance, you get about four- to- six free counseling sessions before it comes out of your pay. But we need other avenues for both working and retired first responders – some kind of relief, compensation, or program. Among cops and firemen, the divorce, alcoholism, and suicide rate is extremely high. Let's be honest: we all carry heavy emotional baggage well into retirement. Throughout the process of writing this book, no matter how many times I sat down to talk about my career and the calls I've run, I teared up. To this day, I cry about many of them because they still affect me deeply.

We need programs to help us navigate our way through the emotional, psychological, and spiritual damage. While you're working in the fire department, they send a CISD (Critical Incident Stress Debriefing) group to your station for stress debriefings. The problem is, you don't really want to talk about your personal problems in front of a group of people. Yes, you can have a private session – they'll tell you to call if you need one-on-one counseling – but if one of them shows up at your station, everybody knows what's going on.

I've discussed often how children are the worst cases you can ever handle. I've carried babies out to the rig several times to protect my crew from the damaging and distracting sounds of hysterical parents, family, and friends. I know it's their child, and I'm not trying to be harsh. Running to the rig with a baby whose arms are flapping backwards, trying to do compressions while looking into their dead eyes is an unforgettable experience. As a first responder, it haunts you forever. But no matter the situation, you don't forget the voices you hear. You don't forget the sounds. You don't forget the smells.

When I attended fire school back in the 80s, they never told me I'd be picking up dead bodies. They never explained that I'd see dismembered people or hear the gut-wrenching screams of mothers and children. No one taught us how to deal with the stress and the emotional toll of the job. They don't require you to take a course where an experienced teacher speaks to you frankly about what you can expect to see and how to cope with it. Maybe I was naïve in thinking I wasn't going to experience these things, but it wasn't what I expected.

Then one day, you'll run your first nasty call and question yourself as you stand there, "Is this really what I want to do?"

In some cases, the answer is yes; in others, it's no.

In my fire department career, I have served with wonderful women. The difference between a man and a woman – not just in the fire service – is that a woman has to prove herself every day while a man only has to do it once. I would go to hell with many of my sisters over my brothers. However, I once worked with a woman who could not remain calm on tough calls. She would do the *dance of the wood nymph*, a term aptly coined by Iron Mike. As soon as we'd arrive on-scene for a horrific call, she'd take quick little steps while waving her arms frantically. One time, she even abandoned me in a nursing home fire, leaving me alone in heavy smoke conditions to extinguish the flames myself.

We'd arrived to find thick smoke pouring out of the utility room and multiple patients in harm's way. Visibility was nil as we advanced the hose line to the front door of the structure in the intense heat. Once we entered the building, I began a primary search while dragging the hose. I'd made it about three feet in when I noticed I was by myself. I continued with a right-hand search and backtracked a little to see where she was, but she had exited the building. Eventually, I found my way to the seat of the fire, which I extinguished. After I got back outside, a lieutenant asked if I was alright. He'd told me he'd seen her and inquired about me. "He's in there," she had answered, pointing to the smoke-filled room.

"You left him?"

"Yes."

He'd told her to go sit on the truck. As we talked, he advised me to file a report about the incident, which resulted in her having to serve under Iron Mike for six months. Per our rules, you just can't fire somebody; you have to give them an opportunity to learn, especially if they're new. Mike was the one for the job because he was one of the hardest lieutenants to work for and brutally honest. In the end, they let her go. There's no shame in it; it's just the realization is that you're not cut out for this kind of work.

Certain times of the year bring me back to particular cases. I once ran a call for a brutal car crash in November, so whenever Thanksgiving time rolls around, it comes back to me in gory detail. Or when January brings its sunny, cool days to Florida, it creates the perfect scenario for remembering the jet ski accident I discussed in the prologue. Because I live beachside, I can see the sun hit the river at a certain point and travel back to that call in 1992 when a young girl lost her life in a tragic accident. Or if I even hear a name like hers, one that sounds like Shauna, I automatically think of her.

Just driving by a dead animal in the road transports me in time to one of the worst calls I answered and the distorted dead body I saw. I remember. And the oppressive emotion doesn't just weigh on you; it weighs on your spouse and children. If you're even considering this profession, you must have a heads-up about it. Active firemen who are struggling to cope need somebody to step up and say, "Hey man, you need to go somewhere. You need to talk to somebody." I don't know if a monthly meeting would help but knowing that you have the ability to go somewhere outside of the department would be huge.

How about getting compensation for a scene you've witnessed but can't move beyond? What happens when you just can't go to work anymore, even though you've been doing the job for 15 years and haven't yet hit retirement but this last call has done you in? You got nothing. Six years in, ten years in…for nothing. There are calls that will set you off the road and force you to quit long before you reach retirement age because you don't want to do it anymore.

The best thing about the fire department? Station-wide, there's a brotherhood. And you get through the rough ones with each other. After you run a nasty, shitty call and get back to the station, everyone will make jokes and funny cracks about it to get through the day. Then toward evening time when it starts winding down, you'll think back to it. Maybe you fall asleep, maybe you don't. But the call is always there now, an experience you shared with these individuals – the only ones who know how it actually felt because they were there.

I worked with a medic out of Station 81 who ran some of the

worst calls I've ever heard in my life. How she did it, I have no idea, but she's already out. She didn't even hit her 20-year mark. I don't know if it was because she got married and wanted to have a family or was just fed up with the bullshit. Because in this line of work, there's a severe amount of bullshit.

And it is bullshit for 24 hours.

There's the political bullshit, like somebody looking at your report and saying, "You didn't spell this word right." I mean, there are some nitpickers out there. They will pick apart not the 20 things you did right, but the one thing you did wrong. In this line of work, you don't expect someone to come up to you and say, "Hey man, thanks, I appreciate it." You just want to go home the next day. In my 30 years, I have yet to see a fireman, paramedic, doctor, or nurse show up to work with the intention of doing even more harm or damage than what has already been done. That isn't the point.

Like the two guys who lost their jobs. These medics tried to help somebody who was underage, drunk, and passed out in her room, and her parents had enough balls to sue the county for it. *Why don't you look at yourself and see what you did wrong, instead of pointing the finger at somebody else and trying to hunt down money?*

Three hearings were held. The first two were inconclusive, but during the third, they reworked everything to the point where they could find sufficient cause for termination because the county was getting sued. The father even had the gall to state, "I'm afraid to walk down the street and see a Rescue because they'll probably try to run me over."

Let me tell you something: firemen, police, paramedics…we don't show up to ruin your day. You called us. We're there to do our best to make it better and save somebody, if at all possible. If you failed as a parent, you failed as a parent. Don't blame us for your shortcomings.

Your 17-year-old daughter was drunk and passed out in her room, yet you left her there alone and didn't check on her for hours. Don't blame me. First of all, why is she drunk? Secondly, why haven't you checked on her? And now that it's too late, you call me to try and make your day better? I try to save her life, and you sue me?

That really happened to the two medics out of my station.

The teenager came home trashed and laid down in her bedroom. Even though her parents saw her in that condition, they left her alone. When she woke up, she aspirated on her own vomit. *Hours* later, her parents checked on her and dialed 911. When the medics arrived, there was a doctor on-scene telling them what to do.

The public may or may not be aware, but we are governed by a protocol and a budget that dictates what we can do medically and in some fire situations, and how much money we can spend. Compiled by a medical director who puts his license up for several hundred people to operate under, the protocol offers recommendations to paramedics in terms of administering medication.

Now picture this: here are two medics, already under a ton of stress in that moment, dealing with a young girl, two upset parents, and a doctor yelling out orders while they are trying to get their job done. The parents had called the doctor first, who was now telling the medics what to do. The medics responded that they had to obey their protocol, then handed him a card we carry for these types of situations when a doctor is on-scene. It's known as a "fuck-off card": you either take this call or fuck off.

Here's the card. If you want to take the call, here's the card.

Meaning, if he accepts, the doctor takes the call all the way to the hospital, explains to them what he did, and writes the report. And he takes full responsibility. Or, he can fuck off. Evidently, this doctor took the fuck-off card, but he still shouted out demands.

This incident ended up costing two medics their jobs, but I just can't imagine suing them because they showed up to save a life. They arrived on-scene with the intent to *help*, not to hurt. Aside from carrying around the weight of this young girl passing away, they got fired. Because negligent parents abdicated their responsibilities and wanted to put the blame on someone else.

So, in addition to dealing with gruesome life and death scenarios, we also cope with another stressor: "Am I gonna get sued?"

One guy who worked with me was always worried about lawsuits. We'd tell him, "If you stay within these avenues, you should be fine."

"Yeah, but…"

And he's right. Sadly, in our society today, you can sue anybody for anything.

In my profession, I have to make tough decisions, like passing by somebody who's dying or dead to get to the one who's salvageable. And it's not based on who's black, white, Hispanic, Asian or anything else; it's based on who can I possibly save, according to the severity of the trauma. Either I can help you or I can't.

You'll have a patient laying there having a heart attack, which is an extended amount of care, and some other ones who have less serious wounds where I can handle one and move on. But if I commit to the guy having the heart attack, he's got me tied up for an indefinite amount of time. One guy can kill four as opposed to if he dies, I can save four. Yes, you have to make choices like that in the street.

But now, when you make your choices, who's going to sue you?

In my personal relationships, there was a time when I became cold for a while. Earlier, I referenced the moment when I accidentally shut my daughter's hand in the car door, and I was like, *"Come on!"* I went over, opened the door, and yanked it out, completely indifferent to her pain. As she cried, I told her to move and bend her fingers while exhorting her to "get over it!" Then, I caught myself and thought, *wow, what an asshole.* I hugged her, but there was really no way to make up for my actions in that moment. I couldn't make it right. But from then on, I tried to pay more attention.

Before my experience at Ground Zero, in my line of work, I saw indescribable pain and suffering, but I just didn't pay attention to it in my personal life. Even when I had to go to funerals, it was no big deal because I had built a defense mechanism around me where I just didn't let it get to me. That's the way firemen work; you just don't let anything bother you. You can't.

Your wife wants to leave you? See you later.

It's just the way it is. It's a hard way to roll. Yeah, you get cold for a while. The job changes you. It makes you selfish because you're everybody's for 24 hours. *Everybody's.* Anybody can call, and you have to respond. So when you're off, you really don't want to share anymore. *For once, I want to do something for me.* You become selfish.

Because in that 24 hours, somebody might need you to go over and wipe a tear and you'd have to do it. I remember a call we had for an old lady who had fallen. After we picked her up, we realized her house was a mess. And since I've always had the luck and ability to work with outstanding people, on calls like these we would clean the house, cook them something to eat, and make sure they were taken care of for the day. And every once in a while after that, we'd stop by to check on them and just say hi.

That happened more than once, but ours wasn't the only engine company to help a neighbor in need. You know, if somebody had a flat tire on the highway, we'd stop and change it for them. Because it was the right thing to do. And we'll continue to help our neighbors on a daily basis because that's the caliber of the men and women in the fire department.

As I said, I am thankful that PTSD is recognized for the military. But it's not officially recognized for first responders, as far as I know, so people need to understand that the men and women who are fighting the wars over here on this turf should come under the same bill. We need help too. The media and the public look upon first responders as if we're a bunch of robots, thinking nothing bothers us. And that's not true.

On my own, I've created outlets like ice hockey, to help me cope. It's a way to burn up energy and release pent-up frustration. But my experiences as a fireman are always there in the back of my mind. Sometimes they keep me awake at night. Sometimes, I jump when I'm sleeping. Often, the memory of a call wakes me up in the middle of the night in a sweat. I'll shoot up in bed, breathing hard and thinking about how it all went down. Then I'll go back to sleep.

And there are more than a few regrets. You're constantly plagued with questions like, *what if I'd gotten there sooner? What if I'd done this instead of that? What if that young girl hadn't gone out drinking that day? What if her parents had forbidden her to drink or kept her in the house? What if her parents had punished her when she got home and made her sit there with them?*

In answer to the last three, my two medics would still have their jobs. So, yeah. *What if* in this field is a big thing.

And I question God. When you're walking with a baby that's not breathing, you're like, "Why? What's the reason?" My faith is tested when bad stuff happens in my personal life, too. But when somebody young passes, all you can think is, "Why?" You want to know why, but you'll never get that answer. So you resign yourself to the fact that all things happen for a reason. Well, you don't agree because there's no good reason for that to happen. Then you get angry. It's a vicious cycle.

I remember once, out of Station 47, we ran a call where a car had rolled over several times with a baby in it. There was the car seat, outside of the vehicle, just sitting in the road. You have no idea how that guy felt as he approached the carrier with its back toward him. *What did he feel like when he saw a dead baby sitting in it? What went through his mind?* Put yourself there.

That's why I'm writing this book. You need to put yourself there. Don't try to brush it off as if the incidents I've described never happened. Everything I talked about within these pages happened – plus many other calls I left out. If you can't feel what I'm feeling, then feel what the loved ones of the car crash victims are feeling. You know, we've all lost somebody.

I want you to feel what goes on in the minds and hearts of first responders as they answer the calls of their neighbors in distress. That makes you human. If you're reading this and not feeling any emotion, you're not human. Once you do empathize with them, you'll have a completely new understanding about the role of firemen, police, paramedics, doctors, and nurses. And hopefully, a greater respect for those who go above and beyond the call of duty. Helping them secure professional assistance with PTSD would be a meaningful way of thanking them for their service to their communities.

GIVING BACK: COMMUNITY SERVICE, GUNS AND HOSES AND THE WOUNDED WARRIORS HOCKEY CLUB

> "The difference between a successful person and others is not a lack of strength, not a lack of knowledge, but rather a lack in will."
> — Vince Lombardi, Jr.

When you're a fireman, no matter what department you work for, during Fire Prevention Week you're asked do what I used to call *dog and pony shows* at local schools. You go to a school, show off the firetruck, and talk to the kids. One year, I got the orders to visit an elementary school when I was working on Merritt Island. While there, a young girl in a wheelchair caught my attention because she was always asking questions. We got along really well; she loved my nickname, "Spike," the one that everybody called me.

Anyway, she was just a fantastic kid. At one point, when she came up to talk to me one-on-one, I told her, "We're gonna get you out of this wheelchair."

Without missing a beat, she affirmed, "Yeah, I'm gonna walk!"

I don't recall why she was in the wheelchair, whether it was Muscular Dystrophy or something else, but her unbreakable spirit made quite an impression on me. Sometime down the road, I was participating in a softball game with the Miami Dolphins – The Fire Department All-Stars versus The Miami Dolphins All-Stars, at the baseball stadium in Viera. As I walked to the dugout, I heard someone calling, "Spike! Spike!"

I looked up, and there she was, standing on top of it, walking with braces on. It was awesome to see her like that and more than a little humbling that she even remembered me. This amazing girl had battled back and here she was, out of her wheelchair.

Since I had nothing else to give her, I offered her my hat, knowing I could get into trouble for not wearing it. Somehow, I managed to climb up and hug her. Although I cannot remember her name, she impressed the hell out of me. Her upbeat attitude and sheer determination had helped her to overcome her disability and walk. It's one of my favorite "feel-good" fireman stories.

TAKING TO THE ICE

In 2002, I was a member of a roller hockey team for Brevard County Fire Rescue. When the team fell apart after so many years, I transitioned into ice hockey because I wanted to participate in the Annual Firefighter Olympics. Ice hockey is identical to rollerblading with the exception that when you transition to ice, it's harder to stop yourself on the skates. Still, ice is way better because it's faster. And I like the coldness of it. From there, I became a member of the Guns and Hoses Ice Hockey Team, which lasted about four years. It was fun.

That experience formed the foundation for what would eventually become the Wounded Warriors Hockey Club, a team I put together before I retired. Originally, my efforts to say "thank you" to our soldiers was my own personal gig. I'd seen the commercials, the people coming home wounded, and the C-57's filled with the flag-draped coffins. Then one night I had a conversation with my old roommate and friend, Ryan, who is a Marine.

As long as I'd known him, he wanted to be a fighter pilot. When he enlisted in the Marines, he was sort of bummed out that he wasn't one. But to his credit, the night he called he said, "You know, I always wanted to be a fighter pilot, but man, I wouldn't do anything else than what I'm doing right now."

"What are you doing?"

"Do you remember seeing the picture with all of the coffins in the plane?"

"Yeah."

"I fly them home. What an honor. I'm never gonna complain again in my life because that is the biggest honor I could ever do for anybody. I'm ashamed for complaining about it in the first place."

After that, I found a site called Honor the Fallen (www.honorthefallen.org). Before I played a hockey game, I'd take a puck, visit the site and paint the name of a killed-in-action soldier on it. If you haven't seen the 2009 film, *Taking Chance* with Kevin Bacon, I highly recommend it. After watching it, the first puck I did was for Private Chance Phelps. From then on, I got a bunch of pucks and for every game I played, instead of selfishly playing for me, I'd play for them. It was just my way of saying, "Thank you," for giving me the freedom to play a game I love.

One day in the locker room, one of the guys asked what I was doing, and I told him. "Man, that's pretty cool," he said. "Why don't you put a Wounded Warriors hockey team together and just play different things?"

"OK."

So I did. In the beginning, the team consisted of anybody who wanted to join, but we never really had a game until my friend Tony, who plays hockey for the University of Florida, and his brother Freddy, who is the goalie for the University of Florida, agreed to play against our team. Since then, we've competed against other schools, including the University of Central Florida. We've been up to The Citadel, out to Las Vegas for a tournament, and all over the place.

The money we raise doesn't always go to Wounded Warriors. We divvy it up and distribute it to other worthy causes including Special Forces. When the equipment manager for one of the college hockey teams was diagnosed with leukemia, we donated the money to him to help cover medical costs.

Every member of the Wounded Warriors Hockey Club and our sister team, AFTAC (Air Force Technical Applications Center) spends their own money on expenses because we're there to raise funds to support the cause. It's the least we can do to express our gratitude to our military members for allowing us the freedom to play the game.

HONORING THE FALLEN, PUCK BY PUCK, GAME BY GAME.

In 2014, I was selected for the Award of Merit:

"Over the last 25 years, Lieutenant Keith Schneider has been a valuable member of his team, his community, and every organization to which he belongs. A founding member of the Brevard County Fire Rescue Honor Guard, Lieutenant Schneider represents his department with a great amount of pride and dignity, whether stepping up in dark times to honor a fallen firefighter or making public appearances. He is well-respected by his peers and subordinates.

"But going above and beyond does not stop at fulfilling his

Posing with my friend Tony, who plays hockey for the University of Florida.

duties as a firefighter. Lieutenant Schneider has mowed lawns, fixed roofs, and stood by others in the community during tragic times. One example of this is when he responded to a call for an elderly couple with real medical issues. While there, he realized they could not maintain their lawn, so he now helps them with that.

"As a first responder, Lieutenant Schneider also assisted with an urgent 2 a.m. call pertaining to the flooding of water in a resident's home. The entire crew under his command stopped the flood and helped with cleaning and drying afterward.

"Lieutenant Keith Schneider is known to be a man who will always lend a hand and has the ability to balance the need to be a strong officer and a compassionate citizen. He sets guidelines for service that others strive to emulate. It is for these reasons he has earned the Award of Merit."

While it was an honor to receive this award, I'll always consider it my solemn responsibility to guard my every neighbor.

SO YOU STILL WANT TO BE A FIREMAN?

> "The two most important days in your life are the day you are born and the day you find out why."
> – Mark Twain

If after reading to this point, you still want to be a fireman, think long and hard think about it. You're not going to get paid much; you're not going to get thanked much. But you don't do it for either of those things – you do it because you actually like to help people. That's the most important part. Having said that, the real reason you show up for work every day is the person standing next to you. You can bitch about your pay and the job. The person next to you? That's your live and die. *That's* why you go to work every day. It's called a brotherhood. And once you enter into it, you start relating to it more and more.

Something bad happens in your family? Somebody will be there to support you. Out of work for any given amount of time? There will be groceries on your table and money to pay your bills. That's what being a fireman's all about. It's about giving, but also about learning how to receive.

If you've read up to this point and still want to do it, take my advice:

Get used to being hot. As you put your gear on in the middle of summer, especially here in Florida, your inside temperature will probably reach about 120 degrees.

Power through. You'll feel as if you don't have enough energy to finish what you're doing, but you'll find it. And you'll get through it.

Prepare yourself. You'll hear screams, cries, and other gut-wrenching sounds of human misery and anguish. You'll smell and see things you'll never forget. But the one life you'll save makes it all worthwhile.

Stay strong. If you become a fireman; if you decide to take that test, summon your strength and courage. If you're a rookie, shut up and listen to what the experienced guys have to tell you.

Go to school, get your degree. Get all the classes you can. It is the best job in the world.

As of this writing, I'm going back to work to do it again. Why? It's kind of like Super Man taking his cape off – not that I think I'm Super Man or any other Super Hero. But Super Man can't just toss aside his cape and his life purpose anymore than I can stop being a fireman. I missed it. Most of all, I missed the people I worked with and felt a calling to get back into it. So...here's to another 30 years. By the way, I'm starting from the ground up; I'll be a firefighter/EMT on a Rescue, which means, among other things, I'll be running the bullshit medical calls.

Good luck out there. Have fun and enjoy it.

FACTS ABOUT THE FIRE DEPARTMENT – YOUR QUESTIONS ANSWERED

Why did they break the windows open?

When we break the windows, it lets the superheated gases and heat out and allows us to get visibility, which is crucial. We can see what's going on inside the house and put the fire out.

If I cut my hand, need stitches and dial 911, I'll be seen faster if I go by ambulance, right?

As I discussed in a previous chapter, this is not true. We'll walk you right out to the lobby, where you can sit and wait like everybody else. An ambulance is not a taxi; it's an ambulance. It's made for emergency medicine. Stitches are not considered emergency medicine. Keep in mind, time is muscle when it comes to cardiac care. So if we take an ambulance out of an area to transport a Class-3 patient to the hospital when they could've easily gone by car, and someone in that coverage area suffers a heart attack, it means the ambulance that comes to assist and transport them to the hospital must travel a longer distance. In the time it takes to get to the heart attack patient, that person could very well die before the medics or E.R. doctors even get a chance to save them. All because a patient who needed stitches thought going by ambulance would speed up their wait time. Please be considerate of your neighbors. Remember, the person suffering the heart attack could be someone you love.

A firetruck passed me with their lights on, then pulled into Publix. What's up with that?

Well, they have these new things out called radios, which we use to communicate. Via the radio, when we respond to a call, occasionally it gets canceled as we're on our way. Since we're already out, we'll shut the lights off and go to the store. Yes, normally we do bring food from home, but during the course of any given shift, we don't always get back to the station to eat, or by the time we do return several hours later, the food is ruined from sitting out on the table. Often, it's easier to go to the grocery store, grab something, and either bring it back to the station or eat it in the truck. That's why we go to places like Publix.

Why do first responders always block the road?

Believe it or not, some of you are lousy drivers. For instance, Engine 47 and Squad 47 were both hit on Interstate 95 after sitting there for over four hours on a motor vehicle accident. And no, this was not at night; it was in the morning when you could easily see the lights. That's why we block the road; for our own safety and the safety of the patients we're trying to assist.

Why does it take so long to clear an accident and why is the road blocked off?

I mentioned this already, but when someone gets killed in a car accident, there's a mandatory homicide investigation, which means a number of things must be completed: first, the Fire Department arrives to declare the person deceased, then Florida Highway Patrol (FHP) comes on-scene to measure marks and distance, plus examine the damage to things like tires. They look at all kinds of factors during their investigation, which takes time. Lastly, the morgue comes out to remove the body. Then the vehicles are removed, and the road is opened. Depending on the accident, it usually takes anywhere from 2-4 hours.

Is Firemen's Gear Fire Resistant? How much does it weigh and how hot does it get?

No. The gear we wear actually burns, just like the clothes you're wearing now, only at a higher temperature. It's not fire resistant. In the fire chapter, I mentioned that the air in our air packs is regular air, not oxygen. In terms of weight, with an air pack on, the gear probably weighs between 35-45 pounds. Inside, temps can reach anywhere from 120-130 degrees, depending on the time of year.

Why are they putting holes in the roof?

To let the hot air and gases escape the structure so we can make rescues. In the old days, we had to go in blind. You couldn't see anything, except maybe an orange glow, and you had to do everything by hand with search and rescue. Nowadays we have a TIC – Thermal Imaging Camera – that makes it possible for us to see a body in the dark or through the smoke. It's very cool. The advancements in technology have definitely helped.

Why did they bust my door?

Because we needed to get in to save lives and put out the fire.

What happened with that car accident?

The two cars didn't like each other. Seriously, we're there to save lives, not to ask how or why it happened.

Why do people leave Brevard County?

Because they're not getting paid enough. They can easily go to a neighboring county and earn anywhere from $8,000 - $10,000 more. Can you blame them?

ABOUT THE AUTHOR

Lieutenant Keith Schneider was born on Long Island, New York and raised in Fort Pierce, Florida. The middle of three boys, he grew up with an appreciation for family, friends, surfing, and hell-raising until one day on a whim, he and a buddy decided to become firemen. Although unprepared emotionally and psychologically for the tragic and oftentimes gruesome realities of the job, he excelled in his work and earned a promotion to lieutenant in 2001. In 2014, the year he retired, he founded the Wounded Warriors Hockey Club to raise money for various veterans' organizations. He lives in Indialantic Beach Florida with his loyal bull terrier, Rin.

GLOSSARY OF TERMS

1. **crike** - A cricothyrotomy (also zalled crike, thyrocricotomy, cricothyroidotomy, inferior laryngotomy, intercricothyrotomy,coniotomy or emergency airway puncture) is an incision made through the skin and cricothyroid membrane to establish a patient airway during certain life-threatening situations, such as airway obstruction by a foreign body, angioedema, or massive facial trauma. Cricothyrotomy is nearly always performed as a last resort in cases where orotracheal and nasotracheal intubation are impossible or contraindicated. Cricothyrotomy is easier and quicker to perform than tracheotomy, does not require manipulation of the cervical spine, and is associated with fewer complications.[1] However, while cricothyrotomy may be life-saving in extreme circumstances, this technique is only intended to be a temporizing measure until a definitive airway can be established. Source: Wikipedia

2. The Knife and Gun Club: Scenes from an Emergency Room, Eugene Richards, Courier Corporation, October 1, 1995. https://books.google.com/books/about/The_Knife_and_Gun_Club.html?id=QHoid2rLpEUC

3. **PTSD** – Post Traumatic Stress Disorder is a disorder that develops in some people who have seen or lived through a shocking, scary, or dangerous event. It is natural to feel afraid during and after a traumatic situation. Fear triggers many split-second changes in the body to help defend against danger or to avoid it. This "fight-or-

flight" response is a healthy reaction meant to protect a person from harm. Nearly everyone will experience a range of reactions after trauma, yet most people recover from initial symptoms naturally. Those who continue to experience problems may be diagnosed with PTSD. People who have PTSD may feel stressed or frightened even when they are not in danger. Source: Mayo Clinic http://www.nimh.nih.gov/health/topics/post-traumatic-stress-disorder-ptsd/index.shtml

4. Agonal respirations are irregular, gasping breaths, often seen during cardiac arrests. In most cases, rescuers will see victims take these gasping breaths no more than 10 to 12 times per minute; that's one every 5 to 6 seconds. Agonal respirations do not provide adequate oxygen to the body and should be considered the same as no breathing at all. Sometimes, this breathing pattern is called "fish breathing" or "guppy breathing" because of the resemblance to a fish out of water. http://firstaid.about.com/od/glossary/g/07_resp_arrest.htm

5. Hurst Jaws of Life: Hurst Jaws of Life brand includes a full line of innovative cutters, spreaders, combi tools, rams, and power units. http://www.jawsoflife.com/en/rescue-equipment

6. Cribbing: A box crib or cribbing is a temporary wooden structure used to support heavy objects during construction, relocation, vehicle extrication and urban search and rescue. It is commonly used to secure overturned motor vehicles, and debris within collapsed buildings. Cribbing is often used in conjunction with other stabilization equipment, such as pneumatic or hydraulic shoring. Source: Wikipedia https://en.wikipedia.org/wiki/Box_crib

7. A Ram is a hydraulic rescue tool used by emergency rescue personnel to assist vehicle extrication of crash victims as well as other rescues from small spaces. These tools include cutters, spreaders and rams. They are popularly referred to in the United States as the Jaws of Life, a trademark of Hurst Performance, Inc. https://en.wikipedia.org/wiki/Hydraulic_rescue_tools

8. Intubate - To put a tube in, commonly used to refer to the insertion of a breathing tube into the trachea for mechanical ventilation. Source: Medicine.net http://www.medicinenet.com/script/main/art.asp?articlekey=4027

9. SIDS – Sudden Infant Death Syndrome is the sudden unexplained death of a child less than one year of age.[1] Diagnosis requires that the death remains unexplained even after a thorough autopsy and detailed death scene investigation.[2] SIDS usually occurs during sleep.[Source: Wikipedia https://en.wikipedia.org/wiki/Sudden_infant_death_syndrome

10. Smoke inhalation - Smoke inhalation injury refers to injury due to inhalation or exposure to hot gaseous products of combustion. This can cause serious respiratory complications.[1] It is estimated that 50–80% of fire deaths are the result of smoke inhalation injuries, including burns to the respiratory system.[2] The hot smoke injures or kills by a combination of thermal damage, poisoning and pulmonary irritation and swelling, caused by carbon monoxide, cyanide and other combustion products Source: Wikipedia

11. Taking Chance, TV Movie, 2009 http://www.imdb.com/title/tt1019454/

Made in the USA
San Bernardino, CA
22 June 2016